Writing the Successful
Thesis and Dissertation

Writing the Successful Thesis and Dissertation

ENTERING THE CONVERSATION

IRENE L. CLARK, PH.D.
California State University, Northridge

PRENTICE HALL

Upper Saddle River, NJ • Boston • Indianapolis • San Francisco
New York • Toronto • Montreal • London • Munich • Paris • Madrid
Cape Town • Sydney • Tokyo • Singapore • Mexico City

The publisher offers excellent discounts on this book when ordered in quantity for bulk purchases or special sales, which may include electronic versions and/or custom covers and content particular to your business, training goals, marketing focus, and branding interests. For more information, please contact:

U.S. Corporate and Government Sales
(800) 382-3419
corpsales@pearsontechgroup.com

For sales outside the United States, please contact:

International Sales
international@pearsoned.com

 This Book Is Safari Enabled

The Safari® Enabled icon on the cover of your favorite technology book means the book is available through Safari Bookshelf. When you buy this book, you get free access to the online edition for 45 days. Safari Bookshelf is an electronic reference library that lets you easily search thousands of technical books, find code samples, download chapters, and access technical information whenever and wherever you need it.

To gain 45-day Safari Enabled access to this book:

Go to http://www.prenhallprofessional.com/safarienabled
Complete the brief registration form
Enter the coupon code G9M5-5SFL-QJHQ-TLLX-T3NA

If you have difficulty registering on Safari Bookshelf or accessing the online edition, please e-mail customer-service@safaribooksonline.com.

Visit us on the Web: www.prenhallprofessional.com

Library of Congress Cataloging-in-Publication Data

Clark, Irene L.

Writing the successful thesis and dissertation : entering the conversation / Irene L. Clark.

p. cm.

ISBN 0-13-173533-0 (pbk. : alk. paper) 1. Dissertations, Academic. 2. Report writing. 3. Research. I. Title.

LB2369.C52 2007

808'.02—dc22

2006035872

ISBN 0-13-173533-0

Text printed in the United States on recycled paper at RR Donnelley in Crawfordsville, IN.
First printing, December, 2006

To my husband, Bill, my growing family,
and the many graduate students who have helped me learn.

Contents

Preface

WRITING THE SUCCESSFUL THESIS AND DISSERTATION: ENTERING THE CONVERSATION is intended to help graduate students complete theses or dissertations by providing both theoretical understanding and practical instruction. It derives from my experience as a Writing Center director, working with students from a variety of disciplines; from my role as a thesis advisor to students in the English department at my own university; and from workshops I have given in Holland to graduate students in the social sciences. It is also based on research I have conducted with students and faculty at several universities that has helped me develop strategies that students find helpful. Its goal is to help you write your thesis or dissertation with maximum insight and minimum stress.

Theoretically, this book explains how theories of process and genre can provide important insights into writing a thesis or dissertation in terms of function and form. Practically, it offers suggestions for undertaking the various components of the process: reading and engaging critically with complex texts, discovering ideas, writing a compelling proposal, developing and revising drafts, constructing the review of the literature, working with tables and graphs, and using various cuing and organizational strategies to maintain manageability and coherence. It also discusses administrative issues, such as selecting and working with an advisor, maneuvering through graduate committees, and avoiding inadvertent plagiarism.

The "process" approach to composition on which this book is based has become common in the study and teaching of undergraduate writing, particularly in the United States. Whereas in the past writing was "assigned" and students were expected to produce a text or "product" that was given a grade, the process approach recognizes an important truism about writing: It does not occur effortlessly, and few, if any, writers produce an excellent text without a great deal of thinking, drafting, rewriting, rethinking, redrafting, and so on. Yet theses and dissertation advisors often do not use a process approach when working with graduate students. Professors who serve as advisors may have little difficulty identifying (or complaining about) inadequacies in their students' theses or dissertations, but they sometimes do not define rhetorical goals and genre requirements, perhaps because they have not consciously articulated these goals and requirements for themselves or because they feel that they shouldn't have to do so. Given this approach, students are left pretty much on their own to figure out what is expected of them.

Most graduate students, however, cannot "intuit" what is expected in a thesis or dissertation, and because they worry about appearing inadequate, they may ask few questions and embark on the process without a clear sense of purpose. Some are nonnative speakers of English, grappling with unfamiliar terminology and language structures. Many have little idea of what is considered "knowledge" in their field, have only a general notion of a topic they may like to explore, are unaware of what is involved in transforming a topic into a workable research question, and don't know what sort of proposal is likely to be successful. Thesis anxiety causes some to avoid writing as long as possible, engaging in extensive reading and note-taking as an avoidance strategy or procrastinating in other ways. Some develop writing blocks, even if they have never had difficulty writing at other times.

Moreover, even thesis or dissertation advisors with the best of intentions have only limited time to devote to graduate students' writing needs; therefore, it is in your best interest to study the process on your own. *Writing the Successful Thesis and Dissertation: Entering the Conversation* can serve as your guide, helping you gain insight into what a thesis or dissertation is intended to *do* and become aware of how its form derives from its *function*. When you understand the *genre* of the thesis or dissertation and learn strategies to help you write more successfully, you will become a better writer and scholar who is able to enter the scholarly community and participate meaningfully in its conversations.

Acknowledgments

I WOULD LIKE to express gratitude to the many students whose insights have contributed significantly to my understanding of the thesis/dissertation process. Their willingness to write proposal logs and provide feedback about their own writing processes enabled me to understand the thesis/dissertation process more deeply and more personally. I have also been fortunate in receiving invaluable feedback from several reviewers whose suggestions have been tremendously helpful. Les Perelman and Jim Williams provided many useful ideas about how I could broaden my perspective beyond the humanities, and Andrew Newman, an American scholar based in Edinburgh, helped me expand my view to include an international perspective. I would also like to thank my editor, Bernard Goodwin, and his assistant, Michelle Housley, who encouraged me to keep writing, obtained reviewer feedback in record time, and maintained frequent contact. Finally, but certainly not least, I would like to thank my husband, Bill, who helped me construct graphs and charts and whose enthusiasm for this project never wavered, boosting my own occasionally faltering confidence and persistently assuring me that graduate students writing theses or dissertations would find this book an important resource.

About the Author

DR. IRENE L. CLARK is Professor of English and Director of Composition at California State University Northridge, where she is also in charge of the Master's degree in Rhetoric and Composition option. She has published in *College Composition and Communication, Profession, Composition Forum,* and *The Writing Center Journal,* and has written several books that focus on writing and the teaching of writing, including *Concepts in Composition: Theory and Practice in the Teaching of Writing, Writing in the Center,* and *The Genre of Argument.*

Introduction

Writing a Thesis or Dissertation:
An Overview of the Process

MANY YEARS AGO, when I was a graduate student, I found the experience of writing my dissertation difficult, mystifying, certainly stressful—words that many graduate students today are likely to use as well. Graduate school overall is challenging, but writing a thesis or dissertation is particularly anxiety provoking because little or no instruction is usually provided about how to do it. In fact, a report written in 1900 for the Pedagogical Section of the Modern Language Association contains a statement that has surprising relevance to the situation graduate students face today:

> When a man has obtained his A.B. degree, he ought to be able to write his language with sufficient correctness to be responsible in the future for his own style. If he has not thus learned to write reasonably well, he probably never will learn. (Mead xxii)

Written over a hundred years ago, the statement, of course, reflects the biases of its time: that graduate students are, by definition, male; that correctness equals excellence; and that improvement in writing is unlikely after a certain point in one's academic development. But beyond these obviously outdated assumptions, the report implies several equally misconceived notions about graduate student writing that explains the persistence of the "sink or swim" approach to writing that many graduate students encounter:

- Graduate students should be able to write a thesis or dissertation without further instruction in writing.
- Previous coursework adequately prepares students for writing a thesis or dissertation—that is, students who have successfully written seminar papers will be able to locate a suitable topic, craft an effective proposal, and develop it successfully with relatively little difficulty.

These assumptions have never been true. Recalling my own experience in graduate school and having worked with graduate students across the curriculum on theses and dissertations, I am well aware of how difficult the process can be. But I also know that when students understand that scholarly work involves interacting with members of a community and that a thesis or dissertation involves *entering the conversations* of that community, they are able to move through the process with less difficulty.

The Rationale for This Book

The 1900 report for the MLA predates the "process" approach to composition, an approach that recognizes that learning to write in an unfamiliar scene or context usually does not occur without helpful feedback and extensive revision. However, that approach is rarely used in working with graduate students. As Sullivan notes,

> Most graduate faculty assume that graduate students, by definition, "already know how to write," and thus writing assumes a secondary and often marginal role in graduate education. The written product, but not the writing process, compels the attention of graduate faculty. ... Despite development of theories which emphasize the processes and contexts of interpretation, we are still tied to current-traditional modes of writing instruction. (285)

Sullivan maintains that the process through which students are "taught" (or not taught) to write a thesis or dissertation completely ignores recent research in composition, with its emphasis on process, multiple drafts, rhetorical goals, and community, and adheres to a remarkably old-fashioned current-traditional paradigm. To write within that paradigm means that students are expected to know intuitively what is required of them; if they don't know, they are, by definition, "unqualified" for graduate work.

Most graduate students, however, have a great deal of difficulty figuring things out on their own and need additional instruction and support. This book is intended to fulfill that need.

A Genre Approach to the Thesis or Dissertation

Many of the underlying assumptions of *Writing the Successful Thesis and Dissertation: Entering the Conversation* derive from current rhetorical genre theory, which maintains that the effectiveness of any text depends on its context—that is, that writing is a way of responding to readers within a particular scene and that "genre" is determined by the appropriateness of that response. Although the word *genre* is often understood only as a means of classifying texts, contemporary genre analysis views texts more comprehensively, focusing not only on their form and textual conventions, but, more important, on their purpose and on how components of a text contribute to the fulfillment of that purpose. Thus, the current view of genre conceives of text in terms of *function*. Accordingly, this book focuses on what a successful thesis or dissertation is intended to *do* and on how its various components enable it to fulfill its purpose. It emphasizes that in order for you to enter the disciplinary conversation, you must become familiar with critical issues in your discipline, problematize and focus a topic, and fulfill genre expectations not only in terms of form and style, but also in terms of the goals you set, the role you assume as you write, and the way you conceive of your readers.

The Incorporation of Reading Strategies

The current misconception that graduate students do not need further instruction in writing also characterizes current beliefs about graduate students' reading abilities. Although in some M.A. and Ph.D. programs students may not take actual graduate "classes," students in American programs usually do. There they encounter readings that may be considerably more difficult and complex than those they read earlier in their academic lives. But instruction in how to read difficult texts does not usually occur in graduate classes because of a pervasive but erroneous belief that graduate students already know how to do it. Reading in graduate writing courses is therefore "assigned," but the process of engaging meaningfully with complicated material is not addressed. Although not all graduate students will admit that they are experiencing difficulty, all struggle with the type and amount of reading they must complete in the process of developing and completing a thesis or dissertation. In recognition of these difficulties, *Writing the Successful Thesis and Dissertation: Entering the Conversation* includes a chapter focused on reading strategies that you will find helpful as you search for a possible topic and write a review of the literature.

The use of genre theory, a process approach to writing, and a focus on the interconnections between reading and writing inform the underlying theoretical approach of this book. The practical strategies and instructional suggestions are all founded on this approach.

Overview of Chapters

Chapter 1, "Getting Started," defines *scholarship* as an interaction with a scholarly community, and the *thesis* or *dissertation* as a means of entering a conversation with that community. It emphasizes the importance of understanding what constitutes "knowledge" in a field and discusses various difficulties students may experience in choosing a topic, developing a proposal, and writing drafts.

Chapter 2, "So What? Discovering Possibilities," discusses a number of strategies to help you learn to speak the language of the academy and discover possibilities for a thesis or dissertation. As Bartholomae observed in his frequently anthologized essay "Inventing the University"...

> Every time a student sits down to write for us, he has to invent the university for the occasion.... The student has to learn to speak our language, to speak as we do, to try on the peculiar ways of knowing, selecting, evaluating, reporting, concluding and arguing that define the discourse of our community.

Bartholomae's idea of "inventing the university" was concerned with the difficulties first-year college students experience when they write academic essays, but the point about learning a new language pertains to all novice/expert situations. To participate in the discourse community associated with a particular field, you, as a student, must "listen" to conversations of published colleagues—that is, read deeply in relevant texts—in order to have something that members of the community will regard as "worth considering."

This chapter emphasizes that when you write for a scholarly community, you are, in essence, joining a vast collaboration.

Chapter 3, "The Proposal as an Argument: A Genre Approach to the Proposal," focuses on the proposal, emphasizing that it is essentially an argument that convinces an audience of scholars that the ideas that will be developed in the thesis or dissertation are worth considering. In this context, the purpose of the proposal is to persuade a committee and other members of the academic community that the problem is of significance to the discipline and has not been adequately addressed in previous work, although selected other texts may have discussed it.

In approaching the proposal as an argument, this chapter addresses the tendency of graduate students to construct proposals that contain a great deal of information but no central point. I have read a great many proposals that review relevant research, discuss antecedent texts, cite statistics, perhaps summarize plots of literary works, but develop no main point. Such texts elicit a reaction from readers that can be summarized as "So what?" or "What's your point?" To avoid the "so-what" phenomenon, this chapter distinguishes between issues and arguments and discusses strategies for transforming vaguely conceived ideas into a focused position. This chapter also contains sample proposals with annotations.

Chapter 4, "Mapping Texts: The Reading/Writing Connection," discusses reading strategies derived from current composition and reading scholarship. Particular attention is given to the strategy of "mapping texts," which is based on the idea that effective readers and writers play an active role in both comprehending what they read and writing a text based on that reading. For a reader who is writing a thesis or dissertation, "mapping texts" means engaging with texts not only to comprehend the ideas they present, but also to see *how* they present these ideas in terms of structure and language choice. Mapping texts enables you not only to engage meaningfully with scholarly work, but also to use reading to gain insight into text strategies that you can incorporate into your own writing.

Chapter 5, "Writing and Revising," discusses insights into the teaching of undergraduate writing that you can apply to writing a thesis or dissertation. These include a discussion of writer/reader relationships, strategies for developing ideas, and suggestions for planning, organizing, and revising various drafts. To facilitate revision, this chapter includes a number of worksheets that you can use, including a "Function" worksheet that you can use both to examine scholarly texts and to revise drafts.

Chapter 6, "Writing the Literature Review," presents the literature review in terms of genre, focusing on the function of the review and suggesting possibilities for organizing it.

Chapter 7, "Using Visual Materials," presents a number of suggestions for using visual materials to enrich the thesis or dissertation. Many theses and dissertations require the use of statistical materials produced in graphs, figures, tables, and charts, but students often do not know how to use them effectively. This chapter presents several possibilities for using visual and numerical material for enhancing the argument of your thesis or dissertation. It also includes examples of what *not* to do.

Chapter 8, "The Advisor and Thesis/Dissertation Committee," discusses the advisor's role in the thesis/dissertation process and the importance of choosing the right person. Stressing the importance of mutual understanding of advisor-student roles, the chapter suggests that, aside from providing guidance and support, an effective advisor can raise student consciousness about what is involved in planning a large text project, particularly setting realistic goals, developing efficient research strategies, and reviewing relevant literature.

In addition, this chapter addresses potential administrative issues associated with graduate studies committees and departmental concerns. It helps you become aware of the forms of scholarly investigation that are favored in your department and suggest possibilities for maximizing departmental resources.

Chapter 9, "Working with Grammar and Style," addresses these topics from the perspective of rhetoric. It emphasizes that grammar and style are not ends in and of themselves, but that they should be used to achieve particular rhetorical goals. It focuses on the following topics: cohesion, coherence, emphasis, sentence expansion, and imitation.

Chapter 10, "Practical Considerations," focuses on other elements associated with the thesis/dissertation process: writing the abstract, working with human subjects, submitting a thesis/dissertation electronically, and understanding the problematic issue of plagiarism.

This book, then, has several goals:

- To help you understand the thesis or dissertation as a genre
- To enable you to develop an effective writing process appropriate for graduate work
- To improve your ability to read complex texts
- To offer practical suggestions for completing this important culminating task more effectively

In the course of writing this book, I have become increasingly aware of how the requirements of a thesis/dissertation vary according to discipline, institution, department, and country. A thesis/dissertation in the humanities is different from one in the social or hard sciences, and programs in countries other than the United States have quite different requirements from those with which I am most familiar.

However, because this book focuses primarily on thinking and writing, and is based on theories of genre and process, graduate students in many disciplines and institutional settings will be able to adapt its main ideas for their own purposes. There is no question that writing a thesis or dissertation is a challenging, difficult enterprise. In fact, at times, you may feel quite lost as you blunder your way through dense and seemingly endless paths. *Writing the Successful Thesis and Dissertation: Entering the Conversation* will help you find your way.

Works Cited

Bartholomae, David. "Inventing the University." *When a Wrier Can't Write: Studies in Writer's Block and Other Composing Process Problems.* Ed. Mike Rose. New York: Guilford Press, 1885. 134–165.

Mead, W. E. "Report of the Pedagogical Section." Proceedings for 1900, *PMLA* 16 (1901): xix–xxxii.

Sullivan, Patricia A. "Writing in the Graduate Curriculum: Literary Criticism as Composition." *Journal of Advanced Composition* 11.1 (1991): 283–299.

1

Getting Started

"What?" thought the Emperor. "I see nothing at all. This is terrible! Am I a fool? Am I not fit to be Emperor? Why, nothing worse could happen to me!" ... And he nodded his satisfaction as he gazed at the empty loom. Nothing would induce him to say that he could not see anything.

—"The Emperor's New Clothes," *Andersen's Fairy Tales*

WHAT DOES THE STORY of "The Emperor's New Clothes" have to do with the purpose of this book, which is to help graduate students write theses or dissertations? In the well-known tale, two swindlers arrive at the Emperor's palace, claiming that their cloth is invisible to anyone who is stupid or unfit for his job. The reality, of course, is that the cloth doesn't exist. The swindlers pretend to spin, but they are actually spinning nothing at all, well aware that few people, even the Emperor, will be brave enough to acknowledge that they can't see anything. Similarly, many graduate students, uncertain about what a thesis/dissertation is supposed to accomplish and having only a vague idea about how to write one, are afraid to acknowledge their uncertainty, fearing that they will be judged unworthy and unfit for graduate school.

Insecurity is the reason some students, like the Emperor and others in the palace, sometimes *pretend* to understand what for them may be a mysterious undertaking. They ask few questions and begin the process of searching for a topic and drafting a proposal without a clear sense of purpose. Many have only a general notion of a topic they may like to explore, are unaware of what is involved in transforming a broad subject area into a workable thesis/dissertation topic, and have little idea of what a proposal is supposed to look like. Anxiety causes some students to avoid writing as long as possible, engaging in extensive reading and note-taking as an avoidance strategy or procrastinating in other ways. Some develop writing blocks, even if they have never had difficulty writing in other situations.

What graduate students should also realize is that professors rarely receive formal training in teaching writing or in supervising students in research. Presumably, students are supposed to figure things out on their own through a sort of intellectual osmosis between academic minds. Some are able to find an advisor who is concerned about teaching and is aware of students' inexperience in undertaking a large project such as a thesis or dissertation. But many students are not so fortunate.

This book provides theoretical and practical insights into the process of developing a topic, drafting a proposal, and developing it into an effective thesis/dissertation. It also addresses practical issues, such as taking notes, selecting an advisor, and working with a departmental committee. Having worked with graduate students from a variety of disciplines, I have developed a number of approaches to thesis/dissertation writing that students will find helpful. Most important, I have learned that when students understand that scholarly work involves interacting with the ideas in an academic community and that a thesis/dissertation involves *entering the conversations* of that community, they are able to write with less difficulty.

This chapter discusses strategies for beginning the writing process and suggests ways of avoiding the "Emperor's New Clothes" syndrome.

Difficulties Associated with Writing in Graduate School

The fact that so many students experience difficulty in writing a thesis or dissertation can be traced to a number of misconceptions about the preparation graduate students receive before they begin and about the nature of the task itself. Other factors contributing to student anxiety include the entrenched elitism associated with writing a culminating work and unrealistic expectations for originality.

Graduate Student Preparation

Although considerable scholarship has been published over the past 25 years about the "process" of helping *undergraduate* students learn to write, little attention has been devoted to the writing tasks graduate students face. Hence, a number of outdated and mistaken notions about graduate student writing ability exist:

- Graduate students write well enough to develop a thesis/dissertation proposal without further instruction in writing.

- A thesis/dissertation is similar to other papers students have written.

- Previous coursework adequately prepares students for writing a thesis/dissertation—that is, students who have successfully written seminar papers will, with relatively little difficulty, proceed through the thesis/dissertation process, from proposal, to draft, to polished document.

These misconceptions are counterproductive to developing an effective working relationship between a student and his or her advisor during the process of developing and writing a thesis/dissertation because they set up unrealistic expectations for students and minimize the role of the advisor. Most advisors are genuinely concerned with helping students, but they may not know *how* to teach writing, particularly the writing of a long scholarly work such as a thesis/dissertation. As a result, although advisors may have little difficulty identifying (or complaining about) inadequacies in a thesis/dissertation, they often do not define its rhetorical goals and genre requirements for their students. Perhaps they have not consciously articulated these goals and requirements for themselves; maybe they feel that they shouldn't have to do so. Graduate school is associated with a lingering elitism in which students deemed intellectually "worthy" are those select few who can discern on their own what is regarded as acceptable. More commonly, though, students begin the process of writing a thesis/dissertation without a clear idea of its generic expectations— what it is intended to "do," what it is supposed to "look like," and what the established members of the discourse community are expecting it to "be."

Moreover, a number of advisors seem to expect students to know intuitively what is required of them because, if they don't know, they shouldn't have been admitted to graduate school in the first place. This is the legacy that has generated the "Emperor's New Clothes" syndrome.

Distrust of Collaborative Writing

Graduate student insecurity associated with writing a thesis/dissertation is partly due to the emphasis in the academic world on the importance of "originality," which is strongly associated with the idea of an autonomous writer working alone (usually in a garret). This legacy of the romantic tradition has persisted, despite the endorsement in composition scholarship of collaborative learning as a means of helping individual writers learn to write. The academy continues to endorse the idea of the solitary author and tacitly supports the assumption that, as Rebecca Moore Howard observes, "some writers are born with 'the gift.' The others can only be socialized not to make fools of themselves when writing—and to revere the writing of the truly gifted" (35). How many of us believe we have this "gift?" My guess is that a lot more of us think that a few others may have it but that we, ourselves, do not. We may consider ourselves hard workers but not original thinkers—and this belief generates insecurity.

Misconceptions of "Originality"

The idea that a thesis/dissertation must be truly "original" can stifle your ability to write because you will find yourself waiting for inspiration to strike, which is likely to be a long, lonely vigil. And yet, what is known about the creation of original works is that they often build upon the works of others, with inspiration occurring within the context of an established tradition or form. An important way to think about creativity is that it can exist only within the context of a particular genre and that a thorough understanding of and familiarity with a genre is a prerequisite for working creatively with it. Thus, Mozart's achievement in the sonata form can be understood as an outgrowth from an established tradition—that is, Mozart had to work extensively within the sonata form before he was able to create an "original" version of it. Similarly, Picasso had to have developed competence in traditional forms and colors before he could create the visual juxtapositions associated with his "original" style. And Charles Darwin, who is reputed to have "originated" the theory of evolution, was working at a time when many other scientists were exploring this same direction. An "original" work often builds on works that are less "original"—and this is certainly the case in the academy.

On the other hand, if you are from a non-English-speaking country or culture, as many graduate students are, your notions of originality may differ. In some cultures, imitation and emulation are privileged over original work, and it is sometimes the case that students incorporate the work of others into their own work too closely. Then they may find themselves accused of plagiarizing, when their intent was simply to show respect for someone else's work. The concept of originality is tricky, so I suggest that you think about it in the context of your particular discipline and raise it as a point of conversation with your advisor and other students.

Differences Between a Thesis/Dissertation and a Seminar Paper

Difficulties graduate students experience in writing a thesis/dissertation also arise from the fact that this culminating work is a different text genre than most students have previously encountered. As a student, you may have written a number of papers in seminars or courses, but, for the most part, the assignments were probably small in scope, well defined, and due at a particular time, requiring you to work intensively on a circumscribed task for a delimited period. In contrast, when you write a thesis/dissertation, it is probably the first time you will be faced with a large, unstructured piece of writing, and it is unlikely that anything in a previous class will have prepared you for developing or managing this kind of project.

The thesis/dissertation is also different from a seminar or course paper, in that it is intended for a broader audience of potential readers. Whereas the audience for a seminar paper is usually defined in terms of a specific professor whose approach to a topic has been expounded over the course of a semester, writing a thesis/dissertation involves addressing a wider and, to some extent, unfamiliar audience. An advisor may be the first person to read your work, but members of a thesis/dissertation committee at your university also will read it. In addition, and of paramount importance, a thesis/dissertation is written for a wider audience of scholars in a discipline who have published books and articles on the proposed topic. No matter what the discipline is, scholarly work involves joining a vast company of thinkers, essentially entering into a large group of collaborators whose ideas inform our own and by whom the thesis/dissertation must be considered worthy. Graduate students, however, don't usually think of their intended audience in this way and may be unaware that unseen readers and listeners are influencing and potentially evaluating their work. As they begin their search for a topic, they don't identify potential collaborators when they craft their proposals and begin writing.

The Necessity of Beginning Early

Misconceptions about graduate student writing ability, the inherent elitism associated with graduate school, concern about the necessity for "originality" in the academy, and lack of awareness of what is involved in locating a workable topic are some of the factors that contribute to difficulties associated with writing a thesis/dissertation. Another is the fact that most graduate students don't begin even to think about their thesis/dissertation until they have completed their coursework[1] and/or passed the necessary exams. Some feel that they are not in a position to consider possible topics before they have immersed themselves in their discipline by taking courses—and, to some extent, this is true. However, it is also a good idea to consider possible topics as soon as possible, keeping alert for potentially useful ideas and texts, and making contact with faculty members involved in relevant research who may point you in the right direction and serve as an advisor.

Discovering a topic is a personal investment that requires intellectual and emotional involvement. If you begin to consider ideas early in your graduate career, you are more likely to "engage" with a topic and find something meaningful to say. The choice of a topic does not usually occur because inspiration, like a bolt of lightening, suddenly strikes, causing you to exclaim, "Aha! Now I have it!" It is more likely to happen when you have been actively seeking possibilities. My experience has taught me that creativity doesn't strike—it *evolves* when one has been grappling with a topic for a while, both consciously and unconsciously. You may

---

[1] *In some universities and disciplines, particularly in the United Kingdom, students don't always take coursework in graduate school. Instead, they work with a mentor or advisor with whom they engage on research projects. Students who write a thesis/dissertation in this setting must begin thinking about a potential thesis/dissertation topic earlier in their careers.*

be thinking about it during the course of a day—in the shower, in the car, while waiting in line at the supermarket—and turning it over in your mind until you find a way to connect with it and make it your own.

If you have devoted significant attention to finding a thesis/dissertation topic, and if you have been mentally tuned in to various possibilities, you will eventually discover a good one. Give yourself enough time and actively pursue the lightening bolt—don't wait for it to come to you.

Certainly, when I was a graduate student, at least some of the problems I encountered when I began to search for a dissertation topic were related to the fact that I didn't engage in the process soon enough. I was so caught up in jumping various academic hurdles before I came to the dissertation stage that I didn't begin to *think* about a possible topic or a potential advisor until the summer after I passed my exams. Then I spent a lot of unfruitful time fishing around, grabbing at various possibilities, scouting around for a faculty member to be my advisor, becoming anxious enough to consider dropping out altogether, and, eventually, after considerable frustration, coming up with an idea that I was able to develop and finding an advisor to help me do so. Until I finally found the right advisor who was able to provide adequate guidance, I bounced around from idea to idea, and the approach I used was absurdly haphazard and inefficient. In fact, it is amazing that I completed my dissertation at all.

An Exercise in Preliminary Thinking

Think about the classes you are currently taking or have already completed. Are topics in those classes particularly interesting to you? Spend some time making a list of possible topics that you may explore further.

Consider also whether you would like to work with certain faculty members. How much do you know about their areas of expertise? What courses do they teach? Can you arrange a preliminary meeting with a faculty member who could potentially serve as your advisor?

Suggestions for Getting Started

To engage productively in the process of finding a thesis/dissertation topic, I offer the following suggestions.

Begin the Process Early in Your Graduate Career

As you complete your coursework, be on the lookout for potential thesis/dissertation topics, for texts whose ideas interest you, and for faculty members who may work with you as an advisor. Perhaps you are interested in the published works of particular faculty members. You should make contact with these people early in your graduate career; make an appointment during their office hours to discuss possibilities. Enroll in a course taught by these faculty members if your program allows you to do so, read their published works, and avail yourself of opportunities to get to know them. Ask more advanced students about their advisors. Has the advisor been helpful and supportive? Sufficiently directive and/or concerned? Reasonably available? Prompt in returning drafts?

Collect Ideas

In addition to getting to know faculty members and being on the lookout for possible ideas, I suggest that you start an "idea file" in a file drawer or box. Whenever you come upon an article that contains potentially interesting ideas, make a copy of it and put it into the file, jotting down a note to remind you of why you wanted to save it. You can also jot down ideas in a notebook or open a file for this purpose on the computer where you can download articles of potential interest. At the end of a year, you will have a rich collection of ideas from articles, books, or lectures that can help you compile a review of relevant literature. One of them could help you discover a workable topic.

Become Aware of Your Own Writing Process

As you begin the process of writing a thesis/dissertation, it is helpful to become aware of the process you have developed over the years as a writer, in order to assess the extent to which it has been effective. As a graduate student, you have written a number of papers for classes, perhaps with great success. At this stage in your career, I suggest that you become conscious of the activities you have performed by responding to the following questions:

- Summarize the process you usually use to write papers for classes.

- How much of the paper do you plan ahead before you begin to write?

- When you write, do you revise immediately, piece by piece, before you write additional text? Do you save revisions until all the text in a particular section has been written? Do you revise at all? What sort of revision do you do?

- What aspects of writing do you find most difficult?

    Generating ideas?

    Developing a main idea or position?

    Doing research?

    Beginning the paper?

    Organizing the paper?

    Providing transitions?

- Are you happy with your writing process? Do you find it effective? Would you like to change some aspect of it?

Reread your responses to these prompts and consider which ones you find most useful and which ones you would like to improve. Find an element in the process that you like the best or find most interesting or rewarding, and, if possible, begin with that one. Beginning with an activity you like at least somewhat can provide momentum for other components of the process that you may enjoy less.

Create a Timetable for Completing the Thesis/Dissertation
Creating a timetable helps you gain an overview of the process, and I recommend that you consult your advisor as you develop it. Does your advisor want you to submit each chapter as you write it? Or should you wait until an entire draft is completed? If your

advisor is willing, I recommend submitting each chapter as you write it so that you can begin obtaining feedback early in the process.

Form a Thesis/Dissertation Writing Group

Although the image of the lone writer scribbling in a garret is a popular fiction, writing entirely on your own can be lonely and intimidating, whereas sharing ideas with others is often enjoyable and rewarding. If possible, I suggest that you form a thesis/dissertation writing group with a few congenial fellow students. Meeting with fellow students on a regular basis will keep you focused on your task and serve as a bulwark against procrastination because you will have to report at least some "progress" to the group or confess that you haven't made any. When you share drafts of your proposal or chapters from your thesis/dissertation with fellow students, they will be able to suggest new directions or note areas that may need clarification or explanation. In addition, when you critique the work of others, you gain insight into your own. Collaboration among writers is usually helpful for everyone, which is why professional writers often participate regularly in writing workshops.

Understand the Thesis/Dissertation as a Genre

The word *genre* appears frequently in this book, and it is important for you to understand how it is used in the context of a thesis/dissertation, In the past, the term was used primarily to refer to the *form* of a literary text, such as a poem, short story, or play. More recently, however, the word has been redefined in terms of *function*—that is, in terms of what it does or accomplishes. As Amy Devitt defines this new concept of genre, "People use genres to do things in the world (social action and purpose) and ... these ways of acting become typified through occurring under what is perceived as recurring circumstances" (698). The thesis/dissertation has a particular function within the academic world; to write one successfully, it is important to understand its "generic" expectations—what it is intended to "do," what it is supposed to "look like," and what the members of the academic community expect it to "be." Thinking about a thesis/dissertation in this way enables you to view it in terms of the audience for which it is intended. When you consider generic features in terms of function, you will understand more clearly the sort of text you are expected to write.

Although theses/dissertations differ by discipline, institution, and country, most adhere to the following characteristics:

- A thesis/dissertation begins by identifying a problem or issue that is well defined and worth addressing. The problem or issue leads to a research question and a consideration of how it may be answered.

- A thesis/dissertation is a persuasive scholarly document that presents an *argument* and supports it with evidence. Its goal is to convince a committee and other members of the academic community of the following:

  - The problem, situation, or issue is significant to the profession.

  - The problem, situation, or issue has not been treated adequately in previous scholarly work (although it probably has been addressed before).

  - The author has created or discovered a credible strategy or direction for addressing the problem, situation, or issue.

- A thesis/dissertation enables the student to enter a scholarly conversation by engaging with other texts:

  - "Listening" to what other texts have to say

  - Understanding their main points

  - Discovering possibilities for expanding or perhaps refuting those points

- Originality in the academic world evolves from the voices of others. Students often become overwhelmed by their concern with finding something completely "new" to say, but a thesis/dissertation often builds on ideas that others have already written about, extending an argument, addressing a gap, or modifying a point of view.

- In terms of the thesis/dissertation proposal, although not all proposals are the same, most devote sections to the following elements:
  - Explaining the problem
  - Showing its significance to the field
  - Showing that the author is familiar with relevant prior publications
  - Explaining the need for solving the scholarly problem in terms of a gap in the previous scholarship
  - Presenting a plan for research
  - Presenting a potential structure for the final written product

Find Examples of the Type of Thesis/Dissertation You Want to Write

The library at your university should have a file of theses written in your discipline, and it is a good idea to examine several to get some ideas for the work you plan to do. Look at how the purpose was presented and at the structure that was used. You may even find one that suits your own goals quite well, and you can then begin by using it as a model. Start by imitating and then move beyond, developing your own ideas as you continue to reflect. Slavish imitation usually results in a mechanical, uninteresting text, but modeling in the initial phase of composing can be helpful.

In addition, the growing Networked Digital Library of Theses and Dissertations (NDLTD) can serve as a useful source of ideas. You also should peruse Dissertation Abstracts Online, which characterizes itself as "a definitive subject, title, and author guide to virtually every American dissertation accepted at an accredited institution since 1861. Selected Master's theses have been included since 1962. In addition, since 1988, the database includes citations for dissertations from 50 British universities." These have been collected by and filmed at *The British Document Supply Centre*. Beginning with DAIC Volume 49, Number 2 (Spring 1988), citations and abstracts from Section C, *Worldwide Dissertations* (formerly *European Dissertations*), have been included in the file (see http://library.dialog.com/bluesheets/html/bl0035.html).

An Ideal Sequence for Getting Started

When you read the title of this section, "An Ideal Sequence for Getting Started," you probably thought that an ideal sequence is unlikely to happen—and you are, of course, correct. Writing a thesis/dissertation rarely goes as smoothly as one would like, and life has a way of intruding on even the most disciplined of students. However, it is useful to consider what your "ideal" sequence may be. The pointers below, derived from the work of Locke, Spirduso, and Silverman, may give you ideas about how to approximate that sequence:

1. Consider why you want to write a thesis/dissertation and what you plan to do when you have completed this project.

2. Locate an area of particular interest that you would like to study on a graduate level.

3. Select a university or research institution that has a strong reputation in the area you want to study.

4. Identify an advisor who has published widely in the area you plan to study and who is known for being an excellent mentor.

5. Work with an advisor to develop a question or hypothesis that will serve as the basis for a thesis or dissertation.

As a way of getting started, Locke, Spirduso, and Silverman make the following distinctions between a "problem," a "question," and a "purpose":

- A *problem* occurs when we become aware of a situation that is unsatisfactory in some way. Awareness of a problem can raise questions, which can then suggest a research direction.
- A *question* is a statement about what you may want to know about the unsatisfactory situation you have identified.
- A *purpose* then becomes the explicit direction for your research. The purpose of a thesis/dissertation is to answer the question you have posed about the unsatisfactory situation.

Thus, "the search for a topic becomes the quest for a situation that is sufficiently unsatisfactory to be experienced as a problem. The proposal has as its purpose the setting up of a research question and the establishment of exactly how (and why) the investigator intends to find the answer. Problems lead to questions which lead to purpose" (Locke, Spirduso, and Silverman 48).

It is also useful to be aware of problems that can cause a proposed area of investigation to be rejected, either by a graduate committee or by another university group that approves thesis/dissertation topics These are the most common reasons:

- The thesis or dissertation doesn't have a main point, thesis, or position. It reviews relevant research, discusses antecedent texts, perhaps summarizes plots of literary works, but makes no argument. It elicits a reaction from readers that can be summarized as "So what?" or "What's your point?" or "Why does this matter?"
- The subject is too broad.
- Key terms are poorly defined or not defined at all.

These suggestions can help you begin the process of finding a topic and writing a proposal. As you move along what can appear to be a meandering and perhaps treacherous path, keep in mind that it is natural to be confused or uncertain some of the time. After all, you have never written a thesis/dissertation before. So have courage! Forge ahead! And don't be afraid to ask questions.

To Stimulate Thinking

Access a thesis or dissertation either in your university library or online that is concerned with a topic in your field. Ideally, it should be a topic you may want to address in your own work. Then respond to the following questions:

- What is the overall purpose of this thesis/dissertation? Where is the purpose stated?

- Examine the introductory section or first chapter. How much information is included in this section?

- Examine the structure of the thesis/dissertation as a whole. How many chapters does it have? How is the content divided?

- Look for the Review of the Literature. Is this in a separate chapter, or is it included in the introduction or first chapter? If so, is it used to justify the topic—to show that this thesis/dissertation addresses a critical issue in your discipline?

- What do you like about this thesis/dissertation? What elements can you adapt for your own work?

Share your responses with a writing group of other students who are working on a thesis/dissertation. What insights have you gained about a possible direction?

Works Cited

Devitt, Amy. "Integrating Rhetorical and Literary Theories of Genre." *College English* 62 (2000): 697–718.

Howard, Rebecca Moore. *Standing in the Shadow of Giants: Plagiarists, Authors, Collaborators.* Stamford, Conn.: Ablex, 1999.

Locke, Lawrence F., Waneen W. Spirduso, and Stephen J. Silverman. *Proposals That Work.* Thousand Oaks: Sage, 2000.

2

So What? Discovering Possibilities

...he took the cover off the dish and saw a white snake lying in it. At the sight of it, he could not resist tasting it, so he cut off a piece and put it into his mouth. Hardly had he tasted it, however, when he heard a wonderful whispering of delicate voices.

He went to the window and listened, and he noticed that the whispers came from the sparrows outside. They were chattering away and telling each other all kinds of things they had heard in the woods and fields. Eating the snake had given him the power of understanding the language of birds and animals.

—"The White Snake," *Grimm's Fairy Tales*

THE ABILITY TO "understand the language of birds and animals" exists only in the world of fantasy, but if you are in the process of writing a thesis or dissertation, acquiring the "language" of the academy may seem equally unlikely. In the course of selecting a direction for your research, presumably you have "listened" to and understood the discussions in your discipline and now have something worthwhile to contribute—an idea, perspective, or question that knowledgeable people will think is worth considering, or at least a direction or a purpose. But how can this be accomplished? How can you discover something "new" to say when so much has already been written? Where should you search? What should you do? This chapter suggests strategies that you may find helpful.

Beginnings Are Always Difficult

The beginning stage of any writing project is usually difficult, and writing a thesis or dissertation proposal is particularly challenging because you are attempting to write in an unfamiliar genre for a new and potentially judgmental community. Whenever writers are faced with a high-stakes writing task, such as a thesis or dissertation, an annoying little voice may begin to whisper anxiety-provoking statements such as, "You don't know anything about this topic. Everything about this topic has already been said. What makes you think you have anything to say?" or even "What makes you think you are capable of writing anything at all?"

A number of years ago, David Bartholomae, in a much-anthologized essay entitled "Inventing the University," addressed the difficulties of writing for a new *discourse community* (a community that thinks, speaks, and writes in a particular way). Bartholomae made the following observation:

> Every time a student sits down to write for us, he has to invent the university for the occasion.... The student has to learn to speak our language, to speak as we do, to try on the peculiar ways of knowing, selecting, evaluating, reporting, concluding and arguing that define the discourse of our community. (134)

Bartholomae's idea of "inventing the university" was concerned with the difficulties first-year college students experience when they write essays for their freshman writing classes, but the point his article makes about learning a "new language" pertains to all novice/expert situations. To participate in the discourse community associated with a particular field, students (the novices) must "listen" to the conversations of published colleagues (the experts)—that is, they must read deeply in relevant texts and thoroughly understand those texts in order to have something that members of the community will regard as "worth considering."

To gain insight into graduate students' feelings and experiences about writing a thesis or dissertation, I asked several in a number of departments to keep a "Proposal Log," an electronic journal in which they could write about how they felt as they moved through the process. The following excerpt is from the Proposal log of a graduate student named Jane, who is writing a dissertation in the field of geography. Jane's statement epitomizes the feelings many, if not all, of us have when we begin to write in a new genre or on a new topic:

> ...the most challenging aspect of writing is getting anything on paper! Having just finished my written exams, I am struggling with staying motivated to return to the dreaded proposal-writing stage. What if I get stuck again? ... What if it is no good? This approach to writing was called my "sandbagging" stage by a friend of mine who watched me during the master's writing phase ... that insight has stayed with me and so I do know that the "woe is me" routine will eventually subside and I will get down to the business at hand.

Jane's entry focuses on the difficulty of getting started on a new writing task and the barriers she erects to avoid dealing with that task. It is an experience that many of us have had.

Brainstorming Activities

To break the grip of immobility that often characterizes the early stages of a new writing project, a number of writers use brainstorming activities to generate ideas about a subject. The idea behind this strategy is that when you have some ideas down on paper, you will at least have something to work with, and a few of those ideas are likely to suggest new possibilities. To begin brainstorming, take out pen and paper or sit down at the computer and write furiously about a potential topic for 5 minutes. Do not stop to revise or reconsider. Just keep writing. Linda's proposal log entry recounts her use of brainstorming as a means of generating ideas:

> My first response is to start out thinking. Thinking and thinking and thinking. Then I free-write. This is really an important process for me because it determines whether I really have something to contribute and if there is a direction I want to take.... I have to determine how I feel about the subject. I need an emotional ante to take me to another level or else I take no joy in writing....

Now I wish I could say that I have this master plan for writing my wonderful essays, but the reality is, they are not wonderful and I have no master plan. My plan is this: Get it all down. Write as fast and furiously as you can.

Brainstorming is a simple technique that many different writers use to begin the writing process. What I like about it is that it can be done anywhere and doesn't require a computer, although, of course, there is no reason that you can't use your computer for this purpose. After you have located a few preliminary ideas, you can begin to look through the research literature—articles, books, other theses or dissertations—to develop your thoughts more deeply. You can also begin to discuss possibilities with other students or a potential advisor.

Keeping a Proposal Log

The proposal log entries of Jane and Linda, just mentioned, were concerned with their feelings about developing a topic for a proposal. But a proposal log can also be useful for generating ideas both at the beginning and throughout the process of writing your thesis or dissertation. As its name indicates, a proposal log is a journal, preferably electronic, in which you write at least once a week about some aspect of your thesis proposal. Entries need not be long (no more than a page at a time) and can be focused in a number of directions. Here are some questions that can help direct your thinking:

Issues concerned with your subject area:

- Describe the subject area about which you are likely to write your thesis.
- What are the central controversies within this subject area?

    See if you can complete the following sentences:

    Some scholars who write about this topic say _____.

    Other scholars who write about this topic disagree. They say _____.

My own idea about this topic is _____.

- How can you position your thesis/dissertation within these controversies?
- What makes this subject area important? Why should anyone care about this subject area?

Issues concerned with writing:

- Discuss your writing process. How much do you plan ahead before you write? When you write, do you revise immediately, piece by piece, before you write additional text? Do you save revision until all the text in a particular section has been written? Do you revise at all? What sort of revision do you do?
- What aspects of writing do you find most difficult? Generating ideas? Developing a main idea or position? Organizing? Revising at the sentence level? Providing transitions?
- Think about a potential audience for your thesis. What knowledge about this topic does your intended audience already have? What contribution to that knowledge do you plan to make?
- Construct a preliminary timetable for completing the thesis.
- Write responses to the following sentences:

  My thesis/dissertation will address the following question:

  It will fill the following gap in the literature:

You can continue to address these issues as you write your proposal log. You can also address any others you feel are relevant, including the following:

- Discuss meetings you have with your advisor. How long do these meetings last? What suggestions did your advisor make in terms of additional work or revision? Were these suggestions helpful?

- What writing activities did you engage in after you met with your advisor?

- If you discuss your thesis with peers, friends, or family members, recount the nature of those conversations. Did they make suggestions that you plan to implement? Were their suggestions helpful?

- How does your personal and/or professional life affect your writing schedule? Do other responsibilities get in the way? Or do they perhaps help structure your time?

You may also want to use a blog or a website to collect ideas you are considering. You can then attach online information such as articles or data to the site, enabling you to find what you need easily.

Whatever mechanism you use to generate ideas and amass preliminary information will focus your attention, both conscious and subconscious, on finding a topic worth pursuing. It is the *focusing* that is most important, and you will find that ideas come to you even when you are not directly attempting to find them.

The following excerpt from a proposal log focuses on Linda's difficulty in developing a rationale for her thesis, a difficulty that I often refer to as the "so what" or "central question" of a proposal. Linda's proposal was concerned with a genre analysis of sympathy cards, but, as is the case in many proposals, her initial proposal did not probe deeply enough into the sort of information such an analysis may discover. After consulting with her advisor, this is what Linda wrote:

> In speaking with my advisor last night about my thesis proposal, she asked me to think about two words—"SO WHAT?" I felt I had touched on the "so what" aspect and, in fact, had geared my proposal around the "so what?" and "who needs to know anyway?" So now I need to think about why my purpose did not jump out at my reader. If my reader is not grasping the "so what" factor, I have to ask myself "why?" My advisor mentioned that I did not hit it in

the first two paragraphs. I need to look at my introduction and basically revamp it. What the heck was I thinking? I know that I need to put that in the introduction. That's part of my writing model. How did I miss that? I usually make my thesis sentence the last sentence of the first paragraph. That's what I get for trying to model my proposal after someone else's work.

Linda is a serious student and a competent writer. And yet her proposal did not indicate what insights were likely to be gained by her investigation. However, after Linda conferred with her advisor and explored the problem in her proposal log, she was able to construct the missing rationale, which she framed as follows:

> In a few sentences, I will attempt to define my thoughts about the value of analyzing sympathy cards:

> The value of the study of sympathy cards is that these cards are a window into attitudes and reactions within a culture to dealing with death. The reason this study has importance is that much of the communication surrounding death is a nonverbal and/or silent rhetoric. The sympathy card acts as a bridge to open communication and express a message. Though a sympathy card is not as functional as a face-to-face interaction, it is better than nothing and expresses a sentiment that may never have surfaced otherwise.

The proposal log enabled Linda to address a very common problem: the lack of rationale, or the "so-what" in her proposal.

Interacting with Text-Partners

Academic writing involves interacting with the significant texts in your discipline, not necessarily with the actual *people* who wrote those texts (some of these people, in fact, may no longer be alive), but with the ideas and concepts that are explored in them. The direction of your research indicates how you plan to address those ideas and the kind of conversation you will have to extend the knowledge base of which those ideas are a part.

To understand this metaphor, imagine that you enter a room where a conversation[1] about issues in your discipline has been going on for a long time. Several scholars are debating an issue, sometimes heatedly, and you listen to the discussion for a while until you are able to figure out the major arguments. Then, after considering what others have said, you offer an opinion about issues in your discipline. Your research then becomes your contribution to the topic being discussed. The "listening" part means that you have read the texts that are considered important and understand their main points thoroughly. The "entering the conversation" part refers to the ideas in your work that address these points in some way, either refuting them, extending them, or offering a modification.

In this way, seminal articles and books in your discipline can become your "text-partners"—that is, the texts to which your thesis or dissertation is responding.[2] They can also help you discover ideas that will lead to your main purpose. To understand the idea of a "text-partner," imagine the authors of these articles involved in a "conversation" about your topic. What would they say to one another? What would you say to them? And what would they say to you?

At this point, I would like to emphasize that although I am using the word *author,* I am not referring to the specific real-world person who wrote the text, but rather to the scholarly persona that is embodied in the text. You may know Professor Jones quite well because she lives on your street. You may have eaten at her home and know her husband and children. However, the "Professor Jones" who writes scholarly articles may not resemble the "everyday" Professor Jones at all because she assumes an academic voice when she enters the conversation through her writing. You are having your conversation with the Professor Jones of the text, the academic Professor Jones, and Professor Jones's text—the article itself can serve as a text-partner.

---

[1] *The idea of scholarship as conversation is associated with the work of Kenneth Burke in* The Rhetoric of Motives *(New York: Prentice Hall, 1950).*

[2] *Discussing a similar idea, Anne Sigismund Huff uses the term "conversants" in her book* Writing for Scholarly Publication. *Thousand Oaks: Sage, 1999.*

Using Text-Partners

Scholarship is conversation, not just face-to-face or electronic; it is a conversation that occurs when you communicate through published writing—that is, articles and books. When you write your thesis or dissertation, you will be contributing to the literature in your discipline, and locating text-partners can be helpful during the initial stage of writing the proposal. To work with this strategy, locate three or four articles that you find particularly interesting and that relate to the topic you are considering as the main focus of your thesis/dissertation. Read these articles carefully and imagine the authors of these articles in a face-to-face conversation. Then complete the following form:

Interacting with Text-Partners

Finding text-partners can be helpful in discovering ideas for a thesis or dissertation. Select several articles that are pertinent to your potential topic. Then, for each one, complete the following information:

Author: _____

Title: _____

Source: _____

The thesis of this article is:

_____

The most interesting ideas in this article are:

Why do I find these ideas interesting?

_____

_____

What aspects of the topic does this article overlook or distort?

_____

If I were to write to the author of this article discussing these ideas, I might say the following:

_____

_____

A potential use of this article for my thesis/dissertation is:

_____

Finding really useful text-partners requires considerable effort. Some articles and books discuss a wide variety of ideas, which may not be directly related to the topic you want to explore. Therefore, it is important to eliminate potential text-partners that address too many ideas. Find those that contribute directly to the topic you want to explore.

When you have found a well-focused set of text-partners, consider what sort of impact your own ideas are likely to make on them. Imagine yourself talking with these "partners." How would they respond to modifications you may make to their central points? What would you say in response? Entering into this sort of dialogue will enable you to discover possibilities.

Finding a Problem

Whatever activities you engage in to generate ideas, the ultimate goal is to identify a problem or issue that needs investigation. When you have located a problem, you will be able to develop a research question that will help you discover the *purpose* of your research. Having thought about your topic through brainstorming, reflecting, and becoming familiar with relevant literature, you should focus on the following possibilities:

- Locating a gap in the literature
- Finding an idea that is generally acknowledged to be true but that has never been established definitively
- Considering an idea that people may think is true but that may not actually be true
- Focusing on an unsatisfying condition or problem that needs to be remedied

Here is an example of how Sally, a graduate student in the field of Rhetoric and Composition, used problem identification to develop an idea for a thesis:

Problem: First-year students often have difficulty understanding assigned reading material and don't seem to be aware of critical reading strategies.

Question: What critical reading strategies do first-year students actually use?

Purpose: The purpose of this study is to determine which critical reading strategies first-year students use when they are assigned reading in their college classes.

Here is another example from a thesis that analyzes several speeches used by world leaders in time of crisis:

Problem: In times of crisis, such as during a war or after the September 11 attack on the World Trade Center, leaders use oratory to mobilize the country. Do these speeches have anything in common?

Question: Is there a genre of crisis?

Purpose: The purpose of this study is to analyze several speeches given during times of crisis using rhetorical genre theory as an analytic tool. This analysis will enable me to determine the existence and characteristics of the genre of crisis.

Sometimes a problem and a research question can arise from your personal affiliation with a topic. For example, Mary, a geography student, noted in her proposal log that she recently learned that her family regularly sent money and other things back to relatives in Guatemala and that they continued to interact with the Guatemalan community in a meaningful way. This continued interaction among immigrants with people in the home country is known as transnationalism. Because her family was associated with it, Mary became interested in this topic. After conferring with her advisor, she decided to focus her research on the impact of transnationalism on communities in Guatemala. Here is how she was able to frame her research question:

Problem: Transnationalism is increasing between Guatemala and the United States, but we lack information about its impact on communities in Guatemala.

Question: How are transnational activities affecting the political, cultural, and economic framework in communities in Guatemala?

Purpose: The purpose of my research is to find out how dependent the receiving countries are on the sending ones in Guatemala.

Exercise: If you have generated an idea for a thesis or dissertation, try to phrase it in terms of problem, question, and purpose. If possible, compare your ideas with those of another student.

Beginning to Write

Whatever strategies you use to generate ideas and discover possibilities, it is important to begin writing sooner rather than later. Some students think that they shouldn't begin to write until they have read absolutely everything on the topic and have a completely formulated idea that they intend to develop. Waiting for everything to fall into place, however, can become an excuse for delay; I suggest that you get started early in the process and use writing to develop additional ideas. There will always be more articles and books to read and more ideas to consider; if you wait for everything to fall into place, you will never begin. My recommendation is that you use whatever strategies work for you to discover possibilities and locate a preliminary problem and research question. Ideas build on ideas, and the process of writing will enable you to discover new ones.

Keeping Track of Materials

When you begin a long-term project such as a thesis or dissertation, you may be concerned about having enough material. But as you continue to do research and collect articles, data, and notes, you may find yourself overwhelmed with information that gets piled haphazardly in various places. As a result, you may have difficulty finding a particular source when you need it. Certainly, I have found myself in the position of searching for various notes and articles that I discover I need as I move through the writing process.

To avoid annoying, unnecessary searches, I suggest that you organize your research materials into separate folders, both on your computer and in paper folders. I also recommend that you combine online and paper notes into actual folders whenever possible so that you can keep everything together and minimize time spent looking for a missing source or page. Some students purchase a special box or file cabinet that they allocate for thesis/dissertation materials. Make duplicates of materials when you can, and create an organizational system that works for you.

As you collect these materials, I suggest that you review them on a regular basis, rereading your notes, considering ideas you may have overlooked initially, and using them as a springboard for further investigation. Being active in your search for a thesis/dissertation topic will maximize the possibility that you will find one that works for you.

Works Cited

Bartholomae, David. "Inventing the University." *When a Writer Can't Write: Studies in Writer's Block and Other Composing Process Problems.* Ed. Mike Rose: New York: Guilford, 1985. 134–166.

PROPOSAL LOG FORM

Most graduation students view writing a thesis or dissertation proposal as a formidable task, different from and considerably more complex than writing papers in graduate classes. Each step in the process may seem unfamiliar—choosing and narrowing the topic, reviewing the literature, conducting research, drawing conclusions, and writing, revising, and editing the text. In fact, to some extent, when you embark on this task, you may feel as if you are venturing into unknown territory, often without any sort of roadmap or guide.

Keeping a proposal log enables you to gain a better understanding of what is involved in the process of writing a thesis or dissertation proposal. The act of writing will focus your attention on aspects of the process you may not have considered and will keep your mind actively involved in developing your ideas.

What Is a Proposal Log?

A proposal log is a journal, preferably electronic, in which you should write two to three times a week about some aspect of your thesis or dissertation proposal. Each entry should be no more than a page long; after you complete an initial set of questions, *you are free to choose your own focus.* However, you can use the questions and ideas listed here to help direct your thinking.

To begin your journal, respond to the following questions in one or two pages, even if you are not sure of your direction or if your thinking changes later:

A. Issues concerned with your subject area:

1. Describe the subject area about which you are likely to write your thesis or dissertation.

2. What are the central controversies within this subject area?

3. How does your thesis or dissertation topic fit within these controversies?

4. What makes this subject area important? Why should anyone care about this subject area?

B. Issues concerned with writing:

1. Discuss your writing process. How much do you plan ahead before you write? When you write, do you revise immediately, piece by piece, before you write additional text?

Do you save revision until all the text in a particular section has been written? Do you revise at all? What sort of revision do you do?

2. What aspects of writing do you find most difficult? Generating ideas? Developing a main idea or position? Organizing? Revising at the sentence level? Providing transitions?

3. Think about a potential audience for your thesis or dissertation. What knowledge about this topic does your intended audience already have? What contribution to that knowledge do you plan to make?

4. Construct a preliminary timetable for completing the thesis/dissertation.

5. Try to fill in the blanks in the following sentences:

My thesis/dissertation will address the following question:

_____

It will fill the following gap in the literature:

_____

You can continue to address these issues as you write your proposal log. You can also address any others you feel are relevant to the process of writing a thesis or dissertation, including the following:

• Discuss meetings you have with your advisor. How long do these meetings last? What suggestions did your advisor make in terms of additional work or revision? Which suggestions were most helpful?

• What writing activities did you engage in after you met with your advisor?

• If you discuss your thesis or dissertation with peers, friends, or family members, recount the nature of those conversations. Did they make suggestions that you plan to implement? Were their suggestions helpful?

• How does your personal and/or professional life affect your writing schedule? Do other responsibilities get in the way? Or do they perhaps help structure your time?

3

The Proposal as an Argument: A Genre Approach to the Proposal

"For mark! no sooner was I fairly found
Pledged to the plain, after a pace or two,
Than, pausing to throw backward a last view
O'er the safe road, 'twas gone; grey plain all round:
Nothing but plain to the horizon's bound.
I might go on; nought else remained to do."
—Robert Browning, *Childe Roland to the Dark Tower Came*

ALTHOUGH EACH ASPECT of a thesis or dissertation can be problematic, writing the proposal probably generates the most anxiety; for many students, the path to writing it seems dangerous, fading into a "gray plain" as one proceeds. In fact, according to research conducted by Mauch and Birch, "the period between the end of the course work and the serious initiation of the thesis or dissertation is a period when most students falter and many drop out" (43). This observation is supported by my own experience with graduate students in a number of disciplines.

What makes the proposal difficult to write? Here are a few reasons, some of which I mentioned in the first chapter in the context of the thesis/dissertation: First, a proposal is unlike other school assignments most students have done before. Second, the nature of the proposal—the length, structure, and purpose—differs according to discipline and particular institution, which means that the requirements of a "good" proposal are difficult to define definitively, even in books that focus on that subject. Third, many students have the idea that a proposal should be original and innovative, addressing a completely new topic or perspective. This idea, in and of itself, raises the task to the level of the nearly impossible. And fourth, but certainly not least, the proposal is a complicated high-stakes task that can have significant career consequences.

What happens when students are confronted with an unfamiliar writing task that has important implications for their futures? From the depths of the subconscious creep the insidious little devils associated with writing anxiety: self-doubt, procrastination, writer's block. Anyone engaging in a high-stakes writing task has encountered these foul creatures. As Lynn Z. Bloom observes, "Although a few writers are equally apprehensive about all papers, short and long, minor and major, as a rule the more important the writing, the greater the apprehension." Bloom quotes from Maya, a specialist in medieval literature, who has been working on a dissertation for several years. "There's always the fear," Maya says, "that you're not as good as you or your professors thought you were, and that the dissertation will reveal what you'd managed to conceal in your course papers—your ineptitude" (http://jac.gsu.edu/jac/2/Articles/11.htm).

This chapter offers suggestions for proceeding through the proposal stage purposefully so that you don't get lost. Its thematic focus is on the key concepts that inform this book:

- Understanding writing as a process can enable writers to discover a workable topic.
- Scholarship can be viewed as an ongoing conversation.
- The proposal is a rhetorical genre in which writer, audience, and text interact to fulfill a particular function.

Understanding the proposal from these perspectives can demystify the process so that you can develop your proposal more easily.

The Writing Process

Over the past 30 years, scholars in the field of rhetoric and composition have learned a great deal about what writers actually do when they write—from the moment they have even a glimmer of an idea to the delightful day that a writing task is finished. Previously, before significant research about the writing process was conducted, many people, including teachers and students, were under at least two misconceptions. One, as I mentioned in a previous chapter, was that writing was a "gift" that only a few people had. Presumably, these fortunate people wrote easily, whereas those without the "gift" could blunder along but would never really write very well. The other misconception was that writing was a linear, staged process consisting of doing invention (or prewriting), writing an outline, drafting, revising, and editing, a step-by-step set of activities that had to be followed in a particular sequence. That view of writing meant that writers were supposed to know in advance exactly what they were going to write. Then they constructed an outline, wrote a draft, and edited it. This was an idea that sometimes prevented people from ever beginning.

What we now know (and what most writers probably always knew) is that the so-called "gift" is usually a matter of hard work and that the process is complex. We also know that people can *learn* to write, even if writing is not "easy" for them (and it rarely is for anyone) and that ideas can be discovered *through* the act of writing. Most important, we now understand that writers engage in a variety of writing behaviors. Some may write outlines; others never do. Some generate large blocks of text before revising and editing. Others revise as they write. Although for some authors writing occurs in a step-by-step fashion, for many others, the process is recursive or cyclical, often messy. Writers may begin with a fairly clear idea about what they want to write and conduct preliminary research on the topic. But then in the process of writing a draft or revising a manuscript, they may discover a new direction or the need for additional research, which moves them back to the invention or prewriting stage, which leads to more drafting, and so on. There is no single way to write a proposal—or anything else.

Finding a Topic

Finding a topic that is suitable, workable, and interesting can be difficult, and, as I emphasized in Chapter 1, "Getting Started," and Chapter 2, "So What? Discovering Possibilities," it is a good idea to keep alert to possibilities early in your graduate career, if possible. But no matter when you begin your search, the following discovery strategies can be helpful.

Keeping Track of Potential Ideas: Reading, Sticky Papers, Questions, Folders, Blogs, Websites

The thesis/dissertation log discussed in Chapter 1 and the strategy of locating text-partners in Chapter 2 are two strategies that can help you find a direction for your proposal. Brainstorming and free-writing, with which many of you are probably familiar, also can help. Related to these relatively free-range strategies is a system I find useful: jotting down lots and lots of notes as I read, walk, or drive—I always have a notebook or a piece of paper with me, even in my car, because I can never predict when something I read or hear will trigger an idea. Often I have a pad of little sticky paper squares with me, and when I read something that I may be able to use, I scribble a few words that will enable me to recall that idea. Next to those words, I write the statement "use for," followed by a brief explanation of how I think I may use it. I then stick the square of paper to a page in a book or article I am reading, or anywhere I am likely to see it. I find that if I don't write down at least the gist of an idea, I am unlikely to remember it later. Of course, your computer is another useful source for keeping track of potentially useful ideas: a folder, a blog, a website—all of these can be helpful.

In searching for a topic, reading and actively engaging with assigned texts will yield lots of possibilities. Reading actively means that you not only seek to understand the meaning of a text, but that you also interact with it, noting questions and areas where additional work may be useful. Reading with questions in mind can help you find new directions to investigate. For example, in preparing this chapter, I found a number of books that presented an outline of thesis and dissertation proposals, including a list of requisite components. But as I studied them, I began to think, "Models are useful, but will they enable graduate students to write their own proposals? Will they be able to write a proposal simply by knowing about its components? Because proposals differ according to discipline, institution, and country, shouldn't I attempt to probe more deeply? Shouldn't my goal be to help students understand something about the writing process and about what a proposal is supposed to *do*?" Those questions gave me an additional focus for this chapter, and I then found myself reviewing texts about the writing process, looking for invention strategies that could be applied to proposal writing.

As you read, keep in mind the following questions:

- What is already known about this topic?
- What would someone in the field like to investigate further?
- What question can I ask that will lead me to find out more about this topic?
- What method can I use to find an answer to this question?

Finding Ideas in Other Theses and Dissertations

A visit to the library and/or an online search to examine other theses and dissertations can be very useful, yielding a veritable treasure trove of possibilities. Because most theses and dissertations are limited in scope, many indicate the need for further study or implications for further research. In fact, they often specify possible directions in the conclusion. You can focus on theses/dissertations from your own university, or you can search beyond, but I suggest that you begin with topics that you know at least something about. Topics that are brand new may catch your attention, but you are more likely to discover a potential direction if you are familiar with the topic.

Looking at other theses and dissertations offers other advantages as well. If the thesis or dissertation was directed by someone in your department, you may decide to work on a related topic and consider asking that faculty member to be your advisor. Also by exploring completed theses or dissertations, you will gain access to a readymade list of sources to use for the literature review. If the thesis or dissertation has been completed recently, bringing the list up-to-date will then be a relatively easy task.

Replication, Imitation, Originality

Another possibility for discovering a topic is to replicate a study that has already been done in another context or to extend the area of investigation in some way. Imitation and replication can frequently yield results that are quite different from those in the original study. This brings up the tricky notion of originality. Some students—and, indeed, some advisors—have a fairly narrow concept of "originality" in the context of a thesis or dissertation. They conceive of the word *original* as meaning something that has never been done or has never existed. Certainly, your thesis or dissertation should present something that is "new" in some way and make a contribution to knowledge in your field. However what most scholars acknowledge is that research is rarely completely original; it builds on previous research, speculation, and discussion. As Locke, Spirduso, and Silverman note, replication is not the same as slavish imitation:

> [I]n direct replication, students must not only correctly identify all the critical variables in the original study, but also create equivalent conditions for the conduct of their own study. Anyone who thinks that the critical variables will immediately be apparent from a reading of the original report has not read very widely in the research literature. Anyone who thinks that truly equivalent conditions can be created simply by "doing it the same way" just has not tried to perform a replicative study. (50–51)

Another possibility is to repeat a study that is limited in some way, instituting changes that are likely to improve it. Perhaps the data sample was not sufficiently large or was poorly selected. Perhaps a theoretical approach or an analysis that yielded indifferent results in one context would work better in another. In your search for a topic, your thesis advisor can help you understand what constitutes originality in your field and consider the issue of how original a dissertation or thesis must be.

Practical Considerations in Selecting a Topic

In selecting a topic, it is also a good idea to consider practical issues. When you complete your degree, do you hope to obtain a teaching position? If so, will your research provide you with an advantage when you apply for a job? Imagine yourself in a future job interview. If the reviewer asks you to explain your dissertation, will you be able to say that some of the work you have done will pertain to courses you may teach? To supervision of graduate students? To further research so that you will be able to build a solid publication record?

If your research requires the analysis of data, how easy will that data be to obtain? If you plan to use human subjects, can you estimate the time you will need to go through the requisite steps? (Chapter 10, "Practical Considerations," discusses the requirements that pertain to human subjects.) It is useful to construct a timeline for the completion of the degree, and when you write your proposal, it is helpful to keep a completion goal in mind.

Connecting with Your Topic

In selecting a topic for your thesis or dissertation, you may wonder about how much you should invest in it personally. Should it be a topic in which you are deeply involved? Or should you choose one that is simply a way to earn a degree? Scholars differ on this point. Some claim that a significant reason that students experience difficulty with school-oriented writing tasks is that professors and institutional constraints stifle their ability to write with energy and passion, forcing them to write about "acceptable" topics instead of those that have meaning for them. In fact, a study conducted in 1981 by Lynn Bloom traces graduate student writing anxiety to lack of personal investment in a topic. Discussing the issue of selecting a thesis or dissertation topic, Bloom uses the analogy of selecting a spouse:

> It had better be one they love, or it will not survive the stress of intimate association.... [T]oo often the students, lukewarm at the beginning of the shotgun wedding, lose interest and eventually abandon the unappealing subject and perhaps the pursuit of the degree as well. (5)

Patrick Dunleavy similarly traces lack of genuine interest in a topic to loss of momentum in completing the degree. "Most students," he observes, "experience some form of midterm slump in their morale, one or more periods when they lose confidence in their project and wonder if it is worth continuing. If your topic is inauthentic for you, if you are not genuinely interested in your thesis question and committed to finding an answer to it, then it will be all the harder for you to sustain your confidence" (22).

In contrast, in *Completing Your Doctoral Dissertation or Master's Thesis in Two Semesters or Less*, Evelyn Hunt Ogden dismisses the idea of finding the "right" topic for a thesis or dissertation. Her advice is to "[F]orget Interesting, Go for Tolerably Non-Boring," emphasizing that "the basic purpose of a dissertation is to demonstrate that you can do acceptable research in your field. It is not your life's work." Ogden notes that "the first criterion is knowledge, but not 'interest' in a specific area. Surely, doing a dissertation in an area you find fascinating can potentially make the dissertation research more enjoyable; however, making the criterion for the topic 'high interest' can also get you into impossible situations" (41).

Certainly, engagement with a topic is desirable because you will have to work with it for quite some time, and a sense of personal presence will invigorate your writing. But as in the selection of a spouse, it is wise to think beyond initial passion and consider other factors. How important is the issue to the field as a whole? Is it a topic that is currently "trendy" but is likely to die out after a few years? When you apply for a position, will the topic you have chosen serve as an advantage? Or will you have to justify your choice? If your career goal is to enter the academy, will you be able to publish articles, or perhaps a book, from the topic you have chosen? Is there someone in your department who will find this topic worthwhile enough to work with you? These are all factors to consider when you are at the exploration stage. If possible, choose a topic that interests you at least somewhat. But don't overlook some of these practical issues.

Joining the Conversation

How does one join a scholarly conversation? Gary Olson, a rhetoric and composition scholar, conceives of this activity as follows:

> [I]magine a faculty cocktail party in which various colleagues and their spouses are standing in groups sipping cocktails and engaging in intimate, sometimes passionate discussions. After freshening your cocktail, you approach several people discussing the influence of postmodern theory on composition pedagogy. Obviously, it would be considered rude to jump immediately into the conversation that had been going on before you arrived. Basic etiquette dictates that you join the group, quietly listen to what is being said and develop a sense of the larger conversation—both its tone and content—before you begin to make a contribution. The same kind of dynamics attend to the scholarly conversation. (21)

Chapters 1 and 2 suggest several ways that you can prepare to join the conversation, even before you are at the proposal-writing stage. If at all possible, try to "listen" to the conversations of your discipline early in your graduate or even undergraduate career. Many of these "conversations" will be discussed in your classes and through assigned readings. As you participate in class and complete reading and writing assignments, note underlying themes, topics, and questions that indicate the critical issues of your field. Try to summarize the focus of those conversations.

When people ask me what my field is "about" and to explain the critical issues of my discipline, I always have to stop and think, even though I have been involved in this field for quite some time. But the questions and the thinking are worth doing. Why is the field important? What issues are being addressed in articles, books, and conferences? Are there disagreements? As a graduate student, can you answer these questions? If not, can you find answers in some of your readings? Can you raise these questions with faculty members or other graduate students? Of course, I can hear a number of students saying, "Listen. I am working and raising a family while trying to complete graduate-level classes with tons of reading and writing assignments. I don't have time for extra thinking or discussion. I barely have time to breathe!"

No doubt, studying for a graduate degree is a busy time, whether you are taking courses or working on research in a lab. Still, if possible, you will find it worthwhile to "tune in" to what is being published and discussed in your discipline. Who are the major scholars (or speakers)? Can you name the most prestigious journals? What sort of issues do they address? The following worksheet can help you focus on some of the answers to these questions.

Worksheet: Tuning In to the Conversation

In writing, draft responses to the following questions:

- What is the name of your "field"?
- What is your field "about"?
- Why is this field important?
- What issues does this field address?
- What are the prominent journals in this field?
- Who are the prominent scholars in this field?
- What issues in this field generate disagreement?
- What aspect of this field interests you the most?

The Proposal as a Genre

When undergraduate students are assigned to write a paper, they frequently ask, "What should my essay 'look like?'" and "How many pages should it be?" These are logical questions to ask when one is expected to write in an unfamiliar genre, and they are appropriate for graduate students to ask as well. However, students don't usually ask three more fundamental questions:

- What is the *function* or *purpose* of the proposal? That is, what is a proposal supposed to *do*?
- For whom is the proposal being written? For what *audience* is the proposal intended?
- What *role* should the writer of a proposal assume?

When you have answered these three questions, looking at descriptions and models will be more meaningful for you. You will then be able to understand how the structure and length of the proposal helps achieve its purpose.

The Function or Purpose of the Proposal: The Proposal as an Argument

The primary function or purpose of the proposal is to *argue* for the worth of the topic selected for the thesis or dissertation. Its goal is to convince a knowledgeable audience that...

- The project is worth doing.
- The project can be done using the methods specified and the time allotted.

Argument is the essence of academic writing, and in the context of the thesis or dissertation, the proposal indicates to an intended audience that you are acquainted with the conversations of your discipline and have found a way to contribute to those conversations by doing the following:

- Addressing a problem or question that others have addressed unsuccessfully
- Finding a gap in the literature that needs elaboration or clarification
- Conducting a study that needs to be repeated or modified
- Analyzing a text that differs in some way from previous analyses, or applying a theory or analytic tool in a new context

Problematizing is central to the process, and a convincing proposal argues the following:

- The problem, question, or issue is worth considering.
- The problem is important to the profession.
- The problem has not been addressed adequately in the profession, although there probably has been some work done on it before.
- The author has a viable strategy for addressing the problem in a reasonable time.

To make a proposal convincing, the writer must...

- Explain the nature of the problem, question, or issue
- Demonstrate its significance to the field
- Establish that the author has investigated prior scholarship
- Present a means of addressing the problem or question
- Show that the work can be completed in a timely manner

I would like to clarify here that although the words *topic* and *subject* are often used in reference to a thesis or dissertation, these words can be misleadingly broad and ambiguous. A better word may be *focus* or *direction* or *research question*. For example, one may say, "My dissertation is *about* immigrants in Los Angeles," a statement that indicates a broad subject area but does not imply a problem or a question. To problematize that topic and thereby transform it into a direction suitable for a proposal requires asking questions that limit and focus the subject area. One may ask, "Which immigrants do you want to study?" or "Why?" or "What do you want to find out about immigrants?" or "What does the literature say about immigrants to Los Angeles?" A topic such as "immigrants in Los Angeles" needs considerable narrowing before it can become a question that can be addressed in a thesis or dissertation. Perhaps the focus can be on the educational achievement of the children of Mexican immigrants who came to Los Angeles during certain years. The restated direction would then be as follows:

> I plan to investigate the educational achievement of children of Mexican immigrants who came to Los Angeles between 1970 and 1985.

When the problem or question has been determined, you can focus on the best method of investigation to use to find a solution or answer the question.

Another point that needs clarification is the usefulness of finding a "gap." A "gap" in the literature may suggest an interesting direction to pursue. But it may also suggest a direction you *don't* wish to pursue because it is unimportant or uninteresting—a topic that scholars in the field think is not worth considering and that you will find difficult to expand upon if you decide to publish. Consult an advisor if you want to pursue a topic that fills a "gap." You may be digging yourself into a hole!

The Use of PQP: Problem, Question, Purpose

For many theses and dissertations, finding a problem and asking the right question about it will help you find your purpose. For instance, Andy, a graduate student in the field of rhetoric and composition, observed that although teachers in freshman writing courses provide feedback to students in a variety of ways, it has not been established which method is most likely to motivate students to revise. Does the "form" of feedback influence how much a student is likely to revise? Here is how Andy's thinking process could be structured:

Problem: Revision is an important component of teaching freshman students to write. Teacher feedback is supposed to motivate or inspire revision. But it is not clear which method of providing feedback is most likely to inspire student revision.

Question: Which method of providing feedback to student drafts is most likely to generate revision?

Purpose: The purpose of my thesis is to examine three different response methods—written feedback, tape-recorded feedback, and online feedback—to determine which method is most likely to motivate students to revise.

Having clarified the purpose of his thesis, Andy could then discuss the approach and method he would use to find the answer to his research question.

You may find these other purpose-oriented questions helpful:

- What is the relationship between _____ and _____?
- What is the effect of _____?
- What is the cause of _____?
- How has the past influenced _____?
- What is another interpretation of _____?

The Proposal as a Road-Map to the Thesis or Dissertation

Depending on its length, another function of the proposal is to provide a mini overview of the first three chapters. The first chapter discusses the problem or question you plan to address. The second reviews the literature, indicating the point in which your own work will enter the conversation. The third (depending on the discipline and the topic) discusses the procedure or method you plan to use. Imagine a thesis or dissertation committee reading your proposal. Will these people be able to discern what you plan to do? Will you have convinced them that the problem or question is worth addressing, that you have adequately surveyed the literature, and that the method or approach you want to use is appropriate?

The following worksheet focuses on the purpose or function of the proposal.

The Function of the Proposal

1. My proposed topic is _____.
2. The problem or question I plan to address is _____.
3. The method or approach I plan to use is _____.
4. The strategies I will use to convince my advisor and graduate committee that this project is worth doing and that I have done the necessary research are _____.

The Audience for a Thesis or Dissertation Proposal

When you write a proposal, you are essentially writing for three audiences: your advisor, a department committee (in some institutions), and the wider scholarly community. Advisor input is crucial, so confer with him or her frequently and provide a full draft of the proposal well in advance of the due date so that you have an opportunity to revise. The advisor will also be able to help you understand the requirements of the department committee, if your institution has one, because committees can be tricky. As Welch, Latterell, Moore, and Carter-Tod point out, "The proposal seems to be the stage where potential committee members play out their own struggles of hierarchy and power(4), and as a student, you may have no idea that inadvertently you have used a phrase that to one committee member is like a red flag to a bull." Another source of information about what a committee is "looking for" are other graduate students. Successful students can explain how they "did it." Others may recount horror stories of how their proposals were rejected. These stories can be alarming, but they can help you avoid similar pitfalls.

The scholarly community is another audience because your proposal represents your entrance into the conversations of the discipline. You have already been introduced to members of this community in the articles and books you have read. Perhaps you have met some of them personally in your own department or at academic conferences. Perhaps you have chosen the university at which you hope to obtain your degree on the basis of someone whose work you admire. Thinking about the scholarly community as your audience means considering how these people are likely to view your proposal. Would they think the problem or question you are addressing is interesting? Would they be impressed with the amount of investigation you have done and with the care you have taken to fulfill requirements?

Proposal Models

Although the previous discussion pertains to all proposals, the length of the proposal differs according to the university at which you are studying. As Glatthorn and Joyner point out, two types of proposals are common, the *comprehensive proposal,* which is very detailed and is equivalent to the first three chapters of the dissertation, and the *working proposal,* which is much more brief (108). A comprehensive proposal may be as long as 60 pages, providing a thorough discussion of the background, problem, review of the literature, and proposed method of study. A working proposal, particularly for a dissertation, may be as short as 20 pages. For a master's degree, the proposal can be as short as 10 pages, just enough to give a committee a sense of the research goal and a direction for further study.

Your *Role* as a Proposal Writer

The term *role* in the context of writing a thesis/dissertation may seem confusing to you because you don't think of writing as a performance that involves role-playing. Nevertheless, you are no doubt aware that when you write for different audiences, your tone and style differ accordingly. The "you" in a letter to a friend is likely to be quite different from the "you" in a graduate paper. When you author a thesis or dissertation proposal, then, you must assume a particular *role* as a writer and scholar. In fact, to participate in any discipline or, one may say, to enter a particular academic "scene," all writers must assume an appropriate role, "perform" that role appropriately within that scene, and address a rhetorical situation or problem present in that scene. You are, in essence, assuming a particular persona—the public face you are presenting in your writing and that your writing will communicate.

What role should you play in your proposal? Here is my suggestion: Think of yourself as a person who has done significant investigation into the topic, has a clear sense of purpose, and feels confident that his or her ideas are valuable. In essence, this is who you actually are within the academic scene. To get into that role, I suggest that you repeat the following sentences frequently:

- I have done a great deal of research about my topic.
- I have a clear purpose for my thesis/dissertation.
- My ideas are valuable.

Repeat these sentences several times a day.

Of course, as a graduate student, playing the role of this ideal proposal writer may seem false. You may think, "I know I'm supposed to be an expert in this field, but I don't really feel like one. Why should I pretend to be someone I am not?" My response is that although insecurity is natural when one begins any new endeavor and certainly characterizes the whole process of writing a thesis or dissertation, *displaying* insecurities will not help your proposal get accepted. In fact, it may have a negative effect on your readers. The role of proposal writer requires you to mask your insecurities as best you can and to "act" the part of a confident researcher. Of course, you would not want to sound arrogant or overly smug, either. Your authorial role is of a thorough, thoughtful researcher, a person who is genuinely interested in the topic, who has done a great deal of preparatory work, who is confident of its importance, and who welcomes discussion.

How can you present an appropriate authorial persona in your writing? Here are some suggestions:

- Use an appropriately formal academic style. Although you don't want to sound stuffy, your proposal shouldn't read as if you were having a casual conversation with a friend. When appropriate, use complex sentences to project a mature style. Clarity is important, but a simple style will detract from your credibility.

- Use an appropriately qualified style. Because the topics addressed in academic writing are usually complex topics about which it is difficult to develop an absolute position on one side, academic writing is often characterized by tentative language that indicates that the writer is a thoughtful person who is aware of the limits of simple assertions. In making your statements, then, use words such as *may, seems,* and *suggests* to indicate that, as a scholar, you understand the complexity of the problem you are addressing. Resist the temptation to make bold, unqualified statements, such as, "The fact that fewer women enter scientific fields is due to gender bias." A more appropriate phrasing of this idea in a thesis/dissertation is, "The fact that fewer women enter scientific fields may be due to gender bias."

- Clarify and document your statements. Although popular literature is often characterized by general statements such as, "Working women have difficulty managing their domestic and professional lives," scholarly literature is characterized by specific information documented by evidence. A scholarly rephrasing of the previous statement would be, "A study conducted by the Falk Foundation of 2,000 female nurses and physicians suggests that working women often have difficulty balancing their domestic and professional lives" (Johnson 78).

Projecting the role or persona of a careful scholar will lend needed credibility to your proposal.

The question of "role" leads to the question of whether it is appropriate to use "I" in a proposal and of how much "you," the everyday, actual person, should be a strong presence in the text.

The answer to that question is, "It depends on where you are." A number of institutions, particularly those in New Zealand, Australia, and the United Kingdom, prefer to avoid personal language and strictly adhere to a third-person, "objective" voice. In the United States, there seems to be more flexibility. In my own university, for example, the judicious use of "I" in a proposal is acceptable, although personal anecdotes or reflections are usually viewed as irrelevant. Refrain from introducing your proposal with a history of how you came to choose your topic and its personal associations for you. The proposal is, after all, an academic genre, and most academic writing is characterized by argument, research, and an attempt at objectivity, even when you have a personal interest in your topic.

Components of the Proposal

If you view the proposal as a genre and understand how elements such as function, audience, and role contribute to it, you will be able to address structural elements with greater insight and to use models effectively. As with all genres, the proposal is expected to adhere to a particular structure and to include particular elements, although the length and scope of the proposal can vary a great deal. In some universities, students are expected to submit only a short prospectus to a committee. In others, a detailed plan of many pages is expected. Such variation makes it impossible to present a definitive list of components and a structural outline that will pertain in all cases. However, the following discussion of components can serve as a guideline.

Overview of the Proposal (to Keep in Mind as You Write)

A thesis or dissertation proposal identifies a research problem or question. Its function is to *argue* that the project is worth doing in terms of contributing to disciplinary knowledge, that a solution or answer can be found using the methods specified, and that the project can be completed in the time allotted.

Elements in a Proposal

To fulfill these goals, a proposal usually devotes sections to the following:

- Establishing the background and context of the research problem or question

  Members of a thesis or dissertation committee may not be familiar with the topic you plan to address. By establishing the background and context, you are helping them understand why the problem or question you plan to discuss is relevant.

- Explaining the problem, issue, or question set within the context of the field

  What makes this topic significant? What other work has been done on this topic?

- Defining key terms

  Each discipline uses particular terms, which may need explanation or clarification for a departmental committee. Defining these terms will enable your audience to understand their relevance to your project.

- Showing that the proposal writer is familiar with relevant literature

  A solid review of the literature will enable you to "enter the conversation" and helps establish your credibility as a scholar.

- Explaining the approach, theory, or method that will be used.

  Why did you choose this particular approach, theory, or method? What makes it superior to others?

- Describing a likely structure for the final product that will be written and a time schedule for completing the project.

A clear plan for completion indicates your thoroughness in envisioning the project, contributing to your credibility.

Evidence in a Proposal

Because the function of a proposal is to argue the worth of a project, the strength of your argument depends on the evidence you present. Of course, this will vary according to the type of thesis or dissertation you plan to write. If your project is analytic or theoretical, you will most likely be depending on materials from books and articles as your predominant means of support. If it is empirical, you will be working with some form of data, numerical or verbal; in this case, it is important to explain the source of the data, the method of collection, and the type of analysis you plan to use. Will your data be primarily numerical? Do you plan to use questionnaires, focus group analysis, or field observations? Will you need permission to use human subjects? Analysis of verbal data uses different methods than numerical data, so it is important that you explain the rationale for the method you plan to use.

Andy's Thesis Proposal

Here is an example of a thesis proposal written by Andy, a Master's degree student in the field of rhetoric and composition. Read the text of Andy's proposal, noting the annotations at the right. Pay particular attention to the components of the proposal discussed earlier, and consider the extent to which Andy's proposal is similar to and different from the one you intend to write.

Title: The Student, the Essay, and Teacher Response: How Three Different Response Methods Facilitate Student Revision Choices

Introduction/Background

Until recently, most freshman composition programs across the country followed a product-oriented protocol, whereby students were required to write a single, final draft of each assigned essay. Typically, the teacher would then respond with written comments in the margins and/or on the back of the essay. These comments would provide feedback that explained what kind of errors were found in a particular essay and simultaneously urge the student to avoid making the same mistakes in their subsequent essays. Today, however, freshman composition courses stress the writing process, and students are required to revise their work by writing multiple drafts of each assigned essay. Thus, if today's composition courses are designed to teach students the value of revising their work, writing instructors must become increasingly aware of what kind of feedback may engender effective revision. This thesis will examine three different response methods—written feedback, tape-recorded feedback, and online feedback—to determine which effectively inspires students to revise.

Although a broad body of research into teacher response already exists, much of it focuses primarily on written response and on what types of feedback students find most beneficial. Straub ("Concept of Control") uses a "set of principles" to classify written feedback as either "facilitative" or "directive" and suggests that students most preferred comments that offer advice, are framed as open questions, or include guided revision suggestions. Straub's findings, however, are limited to written comments only, a limitation noted by Hodges, who suggests that

The author gives an overview of the background of his thesis topic: the teaching of revision as a process. He sets a context for his research.

The author makes brief note here about the main goal of his research.

The author explains the relevant studies in the field that contribute to and support his investigation. He then questions the scope of such studies.

although margins provide a place for "good teaching," many of these "conversations" found in the margins often misfire, resulting in written feedback that fails more often than not. In fact, by gathering verbal response-protocol from teachers who recorded themselves on audio-tape while responding to student essays, Hodges discovered that much of what teachers say during the process of writing their comments never reaches the margins or endnotes on the students' essays. In a similar vein, Billings compares what instructors plan as their goals and what they actually write as commentary, and examines how students and teachers make meaning of those written comments.

The author examines the sources that contribute to his research, noting their limitations. He conjectures on how his study will delve into areas seldom examined.

Anson similarly notes the limitations of written comments, arguing that tape-recorded feedback presents a significant alternative. Observing that tape-recorded comments often offer a less impersonal tone than what often appears in written comments, Anson suggests that his students prefer this method to written commentary and that taped feedback may actually foster their learning process.

As with tape-recorded response, the literature that discusses online response is somewhat thin. However, as computerized distance-learning programs gain popularity, more research will continue to explore this relatively recent response method. Hawisher and Moran state that online response, although mitigated by the notion that its intimacy can breed a high level of informality not typically found in written response, is still worth exploring, if only because it is "new territory." They point out that online response is not a time-saving methodology; however, they argue that students respond favorably to this method because, although it is written, it tends to appear more like the spoken than the written language.

The author explains why he is deliberately not exploring one of the common areas of study about his topic—the effect of student conferences on student revision.

Of course, any discussion of instructor response must acknowledge the superiority of face-to-face conferences. Herrington maintains that face-to-face conferencing with students as they work between drafts is a useful vehicle that fosters engaged, inquiry-based learning. Davis and Fulton cite Patthey-Chavez and Ferris's study that traces the positive effects that teacher-student conferences have on student revision. Price and Hollman echo this and argue that face-to-face counseling can assist all students in becoming better writers. Given the general agreement that the most effective method of response is the face-to-face conference, however, this thesis will not explore it. Moreover, time constraints for both students and teachers often make it impossible to hold face-to-face conferences more than once or twice a semester.

The author explains the purpose of his research.

This thesis, then, will focus on methods of teacher response to student writing, other than that occurring during face-to-face conferences. Whereas previous research on teacher response has explored which method students *prefer*, this project will focus on the effectiveness of teacher feedback in terms of motivating *revision*. It will examine which of three different methods of teacher response to student essays—written feedback, tape-recorded feedback, or online feedback—freshman composition students consider the most useful for fostering their revision choices.

Methods and Materials

To assess the effectiveness of the three different response methods, differences between early and final drafts of student essays will be analyzed. By using a different response method for each major essay assignment—e.g., providing written, tape-recorded, or online feedback—the instructor offers the student a chance to argue which method may

The author introduces his methods and materials briefly, noting how he will proceed with his study.

most effectively inspire revision choices. Surveying the students after each round of different response methods will then provide the data necessary to determine which method the student found most helpful.

The project will involve up to 72 participants taken from three separate Freshman Composition courses (24 students per class) taught by second-year teaching associates. Each instructor will assign three essays that correspond to three different rhetorical categories, all of which are constituent components of the Composition program: Comparative Evaluation, Debate/Argument, and Problem Solving. Each essay requires a first, second, and final draft. The instructors will then respond to each round of second drafts by using the three different response methods, and no methods will be used at the same time. Defined more simply, Teacher A will respond to Essay #1 by using tape-recorded response, while Teacher B will respond to Essay #1 using online response, and Teacher C will respond to Essay #1 with written responses. Each instructor will then rotate the response methods according to the rhetorical category of each remaining scheduled essay.

The author lays down the guidelines that he will use involving human subjects in his study. He explains the procedures he will follow and the materials that will be collected and examined.

Surveys distributed to students will determine which method of feedback they feel is most helpful in motivating their revision choices for the final draft of each paper. These surveys will be distributed and collected on the due date for each essay's final draft. Additional surveys issued to instructors will also determine which response method they prefer and which method they feel engenders the best results for the student. Finally, a survey that gauges the students' attitudes toward revision will be distributed at the beginning of the semester and again at the end of the semester, to see if their attitudes have changed after participating in a revision-oriented course.

The author discusses how survey research will be used.

Instructors will use written response in the traditional manner: That is, comments will be written in the margins, and a longer response will appear as "endnotes" on the final page of the student's second draft of an essay. Tape-recorded responses involve recordings of the teacher's voice only. The instructor will return a student's second draft of an essay along with a cassette recording of revision suggestions, praise, and other feedback. Finally, online response requires that the students go online at a specified time and date, thereby promoting an online interaction between student and teacher. This works much like a one-to-one student/teacher conference. The difference is that it is an online conference, and the "dialogue" will be in electronic format, on a video monitor, thus resembling the Instant Message medium so popular with people today. Following the protocol of this study, the online responses will occur after students turn in their second drafts of an essay.

The author gives specific details about the procedures that he will follow in his research.

Analysis of data will focus on whether the difference among groups is significant. Using interval and ratio variables, I will conduct a Repeated Measures ANOVA (Analysis of Variance) test because this will allow me to analyze the differences among the groups. An ANOVA analyzes how subjects within each group differ from each other, and then it compares those differences *among* the groups. Thus, if there are three groups of response methods, I will look at the ratio of the variation of answers among groups, which I expect will be greater (or more significant) than the variation within groups. ANOVAs also provide information on any interaction between any of the groups and the independent variable. (My independent variable is the type—or groups—of feedback, and my dependent variable is the motivation to revise.) Thus, the analysis will show me whether the differences among groups are significant

The author introduces the way he will conduct his analysis of the data. Note that he uses "I" to explain his method.

He gives a detailed explanation of how he will do his data analysis.

enough for me to infer cause—i.e., that one response method motivated revision more than another.

I will also conduct a chi square analysis because this is based on the difference between what is expected to occur and what does occur. For example, if a survey question asks the subjects to indicate what global concerns about their writing their teacher focused on during feedback, I could offer five categories or "cells"—thesis statement, response to the assignment, idea development, paragraph development, and organization—and I would expect that the answers would be equally divided among all cells. In other words, I can expect that 20% of all answers will be in each cell. But the numbers that actually occur in each cell will probably show no such uniformity; this test is designed to measure the ratio of what I expected against what actually occurred.

He explicates a second type of analysis that he will employ.

Discussion

This study focuses on the overall impact that the three different feedback methods have on students and on the effectiveness of trying different forms of feedback. However, it is also important to address the limitations of this study because there is no guarantee that any means of persuasion (including bribery) can inspire a student to diligently revise an essay. A number of mitigating circumstances can contaminate this project. First, although all students are required to write multiple drafts that demonstrate a serious attempt at revision, it is difficult to guarantee that all students will revise with equal enthusiasm. Additionally, the desire to revise may be embedded in the actual essay assignment itself. For example, students may revise Essay #1 more than Essay #2 simply because they found the first essay's assignment more appealing. Further limitations include the varying degrees of "quality" feedback of the instructors

The author introduces and explains the limitations he expects to encounter with his research.

themselves. It is clear that no two teachers can make the same revision suggestions for a given text. Thus, it becomes difficult to determine what separates "good" and "bad" feedback as interpreted by the student.

However, these limitations should not supersede the desire to posit any worthwhile outcomes that may result from this study. I expect that students will choose tape-recorded response as the style that most inspires them to revise their work. This should be followed by the written comments, while I expect that online responses will be the least favored of all methods tested.

The author further explains the limitations of his study, giving examples. He discusses what expectations he has about the outcome of his research.

Whatever the outcome, however, this study will support the university's Composition program in several ways. The most important benefit is that it will help instructors find effective pedagogical choices in their efforts to respond to students' writing. But its further value is that it will enable graduate students to pursue professional goals with greater insight—to continue education in doctoral programs, to accept a variety of teaching positions, or to work in businesses that require writing, editing, and communication skills.

The author explains how his study will contribute to the field of rhetoric and composition, and to the graduate program at his university.

For another full example of a proposal in a different field, I suggest that you look at several online. A particularly useful example is "Continuity and Change of Reproductive Beliefs and Practices in Egypt from Ancient to Modern Times," which can be found at http://oi.uchicago.edu/OI/DEPT/RA/DISPROP/hansen_diss.html. The sections of this proposal are as follows:

- Statement of the Problem
- Scope of the Study
- Previous Work in the Area

- Methodology
- Sources
- Issues to Be Addressed
- Contributions to Scholarship
- Bibliography
- Notes

The Proposal and Non-Native Speakers of English

If you are not a native speaker of English, you are likely to encounter some additional difficulties in writing your proposal, even though, as a graduate student, you have already demonstrated competence in doing scholarly work. A study conducted by Casanave and Hubbard in the departments of humanities, social science, and science/technology documented that the writing of non-native-speaking graduate students is likely to have more writing problems than does the writing of graduates students who are native speakers. The study notes that "these differences were the greatest in the areas of correctness of punctuation/spelling, accuracy of grammar, appropriateness of grammar, and appropriateness of vocabulary; the differences were smallest at the discourse level" (38).

If you are a non-native speaker of English, it is important that you obtain extra help when you write your thesis/dissertation proposal. Most universities in the United States, and some in other countries as well, have writing centers or labs where you can obtain assistance in writing your proposal. If you can afford to hire someone to help with surface editing, you may find the expense worthwhile. The Casanave-Hubbard study, however, is encouraging because it suggests that non-native speakers are able to master the most important elements in a proposal: the quality of the ideas and the overall organization of the topic. Although surface areas of your writing should be addressed as carefully as possible, these can ultimately be edited. But it is your *central purpose* that will enable you to enter the academic conversation.

Works Cited

Bloom, Lynn Z. "Why Graduate Students Can't Write: Implications of Research on Writing Anxiety for Graduate Education." *JAC: A Journal of Composition and Theory* 2, 1–2 (1981). (http://jac.gsu.edu/jac/2/Articles/11.htm)

Casanave, Christine P. and Philip Hubbard. "The Writing Assignments and Writing Problems of Doctoral Students: Faculty Perceptions, Pedagogical Issues, and Needed Research." *English for Specific Purposes* 11 (1992): 33–49.

Dunleavy, Patrick. *Authoring a Ph.D.: How to Plan, Draft, Write, and Finish a Doctoral Thesis or Dissertation.* New York: Palgrave Macmillan, 2003.

Glatthorn, Allan A. and Randy L. Joyner. *Writing the Winning Dissertation: A Step-by-Step Guide,* Second Edition. Thousand Oaks, CA: Sage, 2005.

Mauch, J. E., and W. Birch. *Guide to the Successful Thesis and Dissertation: A Handbook for Students and Faculty,* Third Edition. New York: Dekker, 1993.

Ogden, Evelyn Hunt. *Completing Your Doctoral Dissertation or Master's Thesis in Two Semesters or Less.* Lanham, MD: Rowman and Littlefield, 1993.

Olson, Gary O. "Publishing Scholarship in Rhetoric an Composition: Joining the Conversation." In *Publishing in Rhetoric and Composition,* Gary A. Olson and Todd W. Taylor, eds. New York: State University of New York Press, 1997. 19–34.

Welch, Nancy M., Catherine G. Latterell, Cindy Moore, and Sheila Carter Tod, eds. *The Dissertation and the Discipline: Reinventing Composition Studies.* Portsmouth, NH: Boynton/Cook, 2002.

4

Mapping Texts:
The Reading/Writing Connection

The strategies students observe in reading can become part of their own repertoire for writing.
—Stuart Greene, "Exploring the Relationship Between Authorship and Reading" (36)

BEING ABLE TO READ effectively and efficiently is necessary for writing a thesis/dissertation and for any kind of scholarship. However, when graduate students read scholarly texts for a class or a research project, they sometimes feel as if they are entering a strange country, a foreign landscape, with unmarked paths and roads that are bewilderingly difficult to navigate. As they struggle to find their way, they may wish for a set of directions or a "map" of the terrain that will enable them to traverse its roads more effectively.

This chapter discusses strategies for "mapping" the texts you will need for writing your thesis or dissertation, based on insights derived from reading theory. You will note that it uses metaphors associated with travel—words such as *navigation, direction, terrain, signposts,* and *maps.* Viewing reading in terms of travel can yield mapping strategies that help you derive more from your reading and adapt strategies you perceive in published works to your own writing—that is, you will learn to *read* like a writer..

The Challenge of "Navigating" Unfamiliar and Densely Populated Texts

Most graduate students have been successful undergraduates and consider themselves capable of completing reading and writing tasks without too much difficulty. However, as you have probably discovered, the reading expectations in graduate school tend to be considerably higher than they are in undergraduate classes. The material is likely to be quite challenging, and some of it may presume a background that you do not have yet. You may find a lot of it quite difficult to understand—and there is so much of it! Faced with these difficult and bewildering texts, you may suspect that no matter how much you have read before coming to graduate school, you haven't read nearly enough—certainly not nearly as much as the other students in your department, who somehow seem smarter, better educated, and more articulate than you. You may also fear that no matter how much you read, you will never catch up. How can you manage to read effectively and efficiently when you are trying to complete a thesis or dissertation?

Effective Reading Is Not Necessarily Quick Reading

Ours is a culture that values efficiency, and in the context of graduate school, the implication is that "good" readers are "fast" readers. Advertisements for speed-reading classes abound, and you may feel frustrated if you don't understand an academic article or book right away. Pressured for time, you may attempt to "skim" material needed for a class or for a research project. But when you finish "reading," you may discover that you didn't understand it very well—possibly you didn't understand it at all.

An important idea to keep in mind is that some reading will take a great deal of time and that you may have to read some texts more than once to engage with them and incorporate them into your own writing. Some material, of course, you will want to skim, to get a quick overview of its potential usefulness. But some of it you will have to read slowly, struggling with ideas and leaving some to be understood later. Here, then, is an important concept to remember when you read a scholarly text:

> You don't have to understand every single idea in a text the first time you read it.

Many articles and books presume a familiarity with concepts that, for you, may be completely unfamiliar. Casual references may be made to studies, theories, or issues that you have not yet encountered. Moreover, many scholarly texts are not written for easy comprehension. Although it would be desirable if scholars wrote articles and books with the goal of making their ideas clearly understood, many do not (I sometimes suspect that some are deliberately written to be difficult). You may then have to slog through dense jungles of text, leaving some of it unexplored or only partially cleared. Sometimes later sections will clarify early confusions in the same text. But you may have to renavigate a text—that is, read it several times to understand it fully.

Constructing a Map of a Text

Inexperienced readers often begin the process of academic reading as follows: They glance at the title of a text or ignore it altogether. Then they simply begin reading from the beginning, proceeding step by step, hacking their way through each word and sentence, attempting to understand each idea as it is presented to them on the page.

In contrast, experienced readers attempt to obtain significant information about a text *before* they begin to read—in essence, to construct a map of the text that will enable them to navigate it more effectively. Here are 10 strategies for constructing such a map:

1. Get an Overview of Its Topography

Before you begin reading carefully with the goal of comprehending the ideas in a text, consider whether it is worth exploring. Examine the title, head notes, introductory material, table of contents, and organizational structure. Do these features enable you to view the text in terms of structure and main ideas? Can you perceive its peaks and valleys or the roads that will enable you to navigate? Are there digressions that lead away from the central direction?

2. *Examine the Text for Its Central "Moves"*

In his book *Genre Analysis,* the genre theorist John Swales discusses the importance of "moves" in academic texts as a way of understanding how a text achieves its rhetorical goal of impacting an intended audience. A "move," in Swales's system, can be understood as a "direction" in which the text proceeds to make its point, and when you look at the moves in the texts you read, you will be able construct a map that will help you navigate. The process of tracing the moves or thought patterns in a text can enable you to understand that text more clearly. Also when you focus on how that text works to develop its ideas—to read *rhetorically*—you will gain familiarity with typical text patterns that you can adapt for your own purposes. Reading rhetorically means that you read a text not only to understand what it *says*, but also to discern how it *works*—that is, how the writer structures the text and uses language to communicate ideas and influence readers.

Some of Swales's research focused on moves that are characteristic of introductions in a research article. After he studied many such introductions, he constructed a three-move scheme that he designated the Create a Research Space (CARS) model. This is a diagram of that model:

Move 1   Establishing a territory

Move 2   Establishing a niche

Move 3   Occupying the niche

Other genre theorists have similarly examined texts from the perspective of "moves" and the way in which they construct a pattern within a text. Building on Swales's work, Dudley-Evans analyzed introductions characteristic of Ph.D. dissertations, constructing a model that consists of six moves. His model is diagrammed here:

Move 1   Introducing the field

Move 2   Introducing the general topic within the field

Move 3   Introducing the particular topic (within the general topic)

Move 4   Defining the scope of the particular topic

Move 5   Preparing for present research

Move 6   Introducing present research

(Discussed in Bhatia, Vijay K. *Analysing Genre: Language Use in Professional Settings.* London: Longman, 1993–97.)

Examining the moves in a text will help you understand how the text functions and enhance your grasp of its content. You can then approach reading with a dual focus: to understand *what a text is saying* and to analyze *how it says it.* This dual focus is crucial for working with complex texts, both as a reader and as a writer.

3. Consider the Text in a Rhetorical Context

The concept of "moves" is based on the idea that nearly all texts have a rhetorical goal—that is, they are written by *someone* (the writer or author) to have an impact on an intended audience. Try to determine, then, who that "someone" may be. What sort of persona is communicated in the text? Does this person seem trustworthy? What may be the author's motive for writing this particular text? What central arguments are made? Can you see where the author is "going" as he or she proceeds along the paths of the text?

Because authors write articles and books to join a scholarly conversation, consider the nature of that conversation. Does the title give a clue as to the author's purpose? Does the author want to change readers' view about an idea or belief? Does the author want to clarify an uncertainty or problematize what is usually regarded as a certainty?

4. Situate the Text Within Your Discipline

Disciplines are filled with disagreements, controversies, and uncertainties, and a text often provides the site for an ongoing debate. Can you determine the controversy (or conversation) that a particular text is addressing? In the context of the "mapping" metaphor, can you characterize the "site" of this text in reference to other texts that address a similar topic? Is it left, right, or center? How do you know?

5. Locate the "Sea of Former Texts"—Areas of "Intertextuality"
In "Intertextuality: How Texts Rely on Other Texts," Charles Bazerman observes that "we create our texts out of the sea of former texts that surround us, the sea of language we live in. And we understand the texts of others within that same sea"(83). Scholarly texts are thus characterized by "intertextuality," which can be defined as the "explicit and implicit relations that a text has to prior, contemporary or future texts" (Bazerman 84).

As you navigate your articles and books, then, note the location of this "sea" of intertextuality. What sources does the text build upon? Which ones does it oppose? What insights into the terrain of the text can you gain by noting the works it incorporates? Note instances of direct or indirect quotation and the use of particular phrases or terms.

6. Compare This Text to Other Texts You Have Read
As you read, consider whether this text resembles other texts you have previously "visited." Is it structured similarly, or does it adhere to patterns associated with a particular genre? Or does it flaunt your expectations? As you traverse its roads, does it seem familiar, or are there unexpected bumps along the road, places that require you to leap across a chasm? Comparing a text to other texts in your discipline and, in particular, to those that pertain to your topic, can aid your reading comprehension and is also essential to writing the literature review.

7. Consider Why You Are Reading This Text
As you navigate the text, ask yourself the following questions that explorers probably ask themselves:

- What am I doing here?
- Why should I continue on this journey?

- What do I expect to learn from this text?
- How can I use this text in my research?

8. Create Signposts That Will Enable You to See the Path More Clearly

If it is possible, mark the text as you proceed. Highlight important sections or interact with the text by writing comments in the margin. Take notes that summarize important ideas (see Chapter 6, "Writing the Literature Review"). Signposts can be a helpful guide if you decide to incorporate this particular text into your own writing.

9. Keep Track of Your Own Location as You Proceed

As you move through the text, pause periodically to ask yourself, "Am I learning anything from this text? Has it altered my perspective in some way about my topic?" Pause from time to time to consider the impact of this text on you as a student engaged in writing a thesis or dissertation.

10. Evaluate Your Presence Within This Text

As you read, consider the value of the text you are navigating. Is this a text that you will want to revisit? Does it warrant additional attention? Do you think another trip would be worthwhile?

Reviewing the Process of Mapping a Text

The strategies for navigating or "mapping" a text can be summarized as follows:

1. Get an overview of its topography.
2. Examine the text for its central "moves."
3. Consider the text in a rhetorical context.
4. Situate the text within your discipline.
5. Keep track of your own location as you proceed.
6. Evaluate your presence within this text.

7. Locate the "sea of former texts"—areas of "intertextuality."

8. Consider *why* you are reading this text.

9. Compare this text to other texts you have read.

10. Evaluate your presence within this text.

Mapping a Text: "The Prickly Politics of School Starting Time," by Kyla L. Wahlstrom

Read the article by Kyla L. Wahlstrom. Then note how this text can be "mapped" using the 10 previous suggestions.

The Prickly Politics of School Starting Time

By Kyla L. Wahlstrom

There are many questions yet to be answered about the consequences of a change in school starting time. But one thing is certain: As the transition is being planned and implemented, all the stakeholders who will be affected need to be consulted and kept informed.

Some school districts have responded to recent research findings on adolescent sleep patterns and needs by significantly changing high school starting times. Other districts are considering such a move. But tinkering with the school-day schedule is not without its risks.

Aware of those risks, in the fall of 1996, several superintendents of suburban Minnesota school districts asked the Center for Applied Research and Educational Improvement (CAREI) at the University of Minnesota to assess the attitudes of stakeholders toward such a venture. Seventeen school districts agreed to participate in the study, which soon focused not only on high schools but also on elementary and middle/junior high schools, since the schedules of all buildings in a district are inextricably linked.[1]

Of the 17 districts, only 1 of them—Edina—had already made the decision to start the high school day 70 minutes later in 1996–97 than the previous school year. At the start of the study, then, only the stakeholders in Edina were actually experiencing the change. A year later, the Minneapolis

School District pushed back the starting time of its seven comprehensive high schools by an hour and 25 minutes, from 7:15 to 8:40 a.m., enabling CAREI to study the actual impact of a later starting time in that district as well.[2]

The CAREI researchers discovered that changing a school's starting time provokes the same kind of emotional reaction from stakeholders as closing a school or changing a school's attendance area. A school's starting time sets the rhythm of the day for teachers, parents, students, and members of the community at large. The impact of changing that starting time is felt individually, and the individuals who are affected need to have their views heard and legitimized so that the discussion can move forward in search of common ground. Another striking finding from the first year of the CAREI study had to do with the role that assumptions play in discussions of changing school starting times. Informal conversations on the topic seemed invariably to include a comment such as "The transportation department rules the district, and this change cannot take place because of bus problems" or "The coaches will never go along with this idea—there's no use in even approaching them."

To assess the accuracy of these and similar assumptions, we conducted individual interviews during the first year of the study with each participating district's transportation director, with 51 coaches and co-curricular faculty advisors, with all 17 district directors of community education, with several food service directors, with several district personnel directors, with all elementary and secondary curriculum directors, and with local employers who provide after-school jobs for students. Surprisingly, none of the interviewees suggested that a change in school starting time—especially at the high school level—would be out of the question. Indeed, though coaches and transportation directors did voice some concerns, most respondents in all categories were willing to discuss at length ways of implementing such a change, since it would be beneficial for students and their learning. To allow untested assumptions to forestall debate on the issue is to close the door prematurely (and possibly wrongly) to later starting times for high school students.

The CAREI study showed, too, that advocates for later school starting times tended to use in their lobbying efforts both hard data (e.g., the findings of sleep research on adolescents) and testimonials (e.g., positive outcomes from districts that had already made such a change). In both Edina and Minneapolis, a small number of advocates had a positive impact on the decision-making process.

It's important to remember, however, that strident advocacy can squelch debate. And without thorough discussion of the issues surrounding a proposed change in school starting time, any decision will be shallow and may have to be revisited.

In both Edina and Minneapolis, shifts in high school starting times affected the starting times of elementary and middle schools as well. Had the school board members in either of those districts focused solely on the logistics of the change, it is very unlikely that a later high school starting time would have been implemented. But the school boards in both districts first considered the research data on adolescent sleep needs. To their credit, they posed the question, Are the data of sufficient quality and relevance to merit consideration? With that question answered affirmatively, the next questions became: What do we hope to gain by shifting our high school starting time? And what may we lose in the process? The answers to these two questions had to be based on fact, not on emotion or on potential logistical problems.

Eventually, however, both school boards arrived at the point where concerns about logistics appropriately entered the debate. Then the question became, What will it take to bring our school schedules into line with what the research tells us about adolescent sleep needs? The boards formed several subcommittees to investigate logistical problems and to come up with possible scenarios. Throughout the decision-making process, though, factual evidence took precedence, and students' best interests held sway. As a result, the discussions involved much less wrangling than has been seen in other districts embroiled in the same debate. From a school board's perspective, keeping a potentially divisive debate focused on student needs is good politics.

If altering high school starting times is risky for school boards, it is equally risky for superintendents. In an open forum, the 17 superintendents whose districts took part in the CAREI study discussed the dissension that community debate on the topic had caused in some locales. Three superintendents, in whose districts the topic had not surfaced, said they did not plan to bring it up. Two of the three noted that their contracts were up for renewal, and they did not want their boards split over this potentially divisive issue (on which they would be forced to take a stand). They elected instead to remain publicly silent and privately neutral on the topic.

In Minneapolis, the decision to move to a later starting time for the high schools was made under an interim superintendent. When the new superintendent took over, she "inherited" that decision, and any perceived negatives related to its implementation were not associated with her.

If altering school starting times is risky for school boards and superintendents, it is no less so for high school principals. In Edina and Minneapolis, the high school principals served on the committees that made the decision to push back high school starting times. Like other committee members, these principals had access to the sleep research data and to information on outcomes from districts that had already taken such action. Armed with the facts, the principals were able to refute unsubstantiated claims and to respond to the concerns of students, parents, and teachers. Participation in the committees' debates also helped the high school principals identify potential sources of resistance to the change and learn to deal with them before opposition escalated.

It was equally important to have the elementary and middle/junior high school principals involved in the discussions, since changing the high school starting time inevitably affects other buildings as well. In large districts, however, it is impractical to have as many principals take part in the deliberations as may be optimal. Minneapolis compensated by providing regular briefings on the committees' discussions to all principals in the district.

Clearly, schools at all levels whose own schedules will be affected by a change in the high school starting time must be given sufficient advance notice. In Minneapolis, schools that were told in the spring that their starting times would be changed in the fall encountered much less resistance from parents and staff members than did schools that learned about the change shortly before the fall term began. Staff members and parents need time to adjust their personal and family schedules, and providing such time is one key to a smooth transition.

All the findings of the CAREI study that I have mentioned so far apply to both urban and suburban schools and school districts. But a few factors emerged that seem more pertinent to one setting than to the other.

The reactions of high school teachers to a later starting time differed by setting, for example. A clear majority of the suburban teachers said that they liked the change, for reasons that ranged from "more time to incorporate the news of the day into my lessons" and "more students are awake and fully participating in my first- and second-hour classes" to "more time to talk with fellow teachers about sharing materials and team teaching." The suburban teachers were still arriving at an early hour—but, because of the later dismissal time, they were working a longer day.

Urban high school teachers, by contrast, were evenly split between liking (45.2%) and not liking (45.7%) the later starting time. Those who responded positively to the change cited many of the same reasons listed by their suburban counterparts. But two-thirds of the urban teachers who did not like the change mentioned the negative impact that a later dismissal time had on their personal lives. Their comments ranged from "I feel I have no 'down time' before I go home" and "I have lost at least an hour that I would otherwise spend at my second job" to "I now have to face rush-hour traffic." Only one-third of the teachers who disliked the change mentioned the needs of students in their listings of negative concerns.

These sharp differences in teachers' attitudes deserve further study. Perhaps urban teachers are simply reflecting the stresses of teaching under less than ideal conditions. The personal toll of having to make accommodations for a later starting time may be the final straw that makes this change feel overwhelming.

The preferred dismissal time for elementary and middle/junior high schools is another factor that differs by locale. Parents in both suburban and urban areas worry about young children walking along roads or waiting for a bus at a road's edge in winter darkness. But urban parents worry too that "there's a different kind of predator out there in the late afternoon." Thus urban parents prefer an earlier school dismissal time to a later one.

A third issue that differs by locale is "zero hour" classes—those that meet an hour before the regular school day begins. Such classes are usually limited in enrollment, since they serve accelerated students or youngsters in work/study programs. The CAREI study reveals that more suburban students than urban ones take zero hour classes because transportation to school is less of a problem in suburban areas. This equity issue merits further study.

Moreover, zero hour classes negate for participants the beneficial effects of a later school starting time. Districts may wish to consider the wisdom of offering such options.

Obviously, changing a high school's starting time produces a complex array of benefits and tensions. Just as clearly, districts must challenge the assumptions before a genuine dialogue can take place on the topic.

Meanwhile, we still do not know the effect of a later high school starting time on student achievement. In an effort to provide that information, CAREI is now looking at longitudinal achievement data from districts that implemented a later starting time several years ago.

CAREI will also seek to answer the question of whether a later high school starting time reduces the incidence of juvenile misbehavior by keeping youngsters in school until later in the afternoon. To date, there is no evidence to suggest that crime rates have dropped as a result of pushing back school starting times.

CAREI has studied most extensively the two Minnesota districts that have pushed back their high school starting times by an hour or more. Other districts in the state have implemented a 30- to 40-minute delay in the start of school. Still other districts have accepted the value of a later starting time but are struggling in committees over how to deal with the logistical problems. Meanwhile, CAREI researchers are looking for an answer to the question, How late is late enough to help address the sleep needs of adolescents without changing school schedules more than is necessary?

High school starting time is a seemingly simple issue with prickly political dimensions, and there is no single solution that will fit all districts. Only through open discussion of their concerns can stakeholders develop a shared understanding of the facts that will lead to a reasonable—but purely local—decision. And that's as it should be, since those stakeholders are the ones who will have to live with the consequences.

1. Kyla Wahlstrom and Carol Freeman, "Executive Summary of Findings from School Start Time Study," 1997, available from http://carei.coled.umn.edu.

2. Kyla Wahlstrom, Gordon Wrobel, and Patricia Kubow, "Executive Summary of Findings from Minneapolis School District School Start Time Study," 1998, available from http://carei.coled.umn.edu.

File Name and Bibliographic Information
Kyla L. Wahlstrom, "The Prickly Politics of School Starting Times," *Phi Delta Kappan* 80, 05, January 1999, 344–347.

Here is a way that this text can be "mapped" using the strategies discussed above:

1. *Get an overview of the topography.*

    The note at the beginning of the article refers to questions concerning the "consequences of a change in school starting" and the word *stakeholders*. These phrases suggest that the article is concerned with opinions by stakeholders about a proposed change in school starting time. The note at the beginning of the article indicates that the author was associate director of the Center for Applied Research and Educational Improvement, University of Minnesota, Minneapolis, indicating that this is a research report that presents findings about this topic. Note that the introduction to the article also provides an overview of what the study was about: the questioning of 17 school districts in Minnesota about attitudes concerning a later starting time for high schools.

2. *Examine the text for its central moves.*

    This text has no headings or subheadings, so to get a sense of the central moves, one needs to skim the text. The introduction provides an overview of what the study involved and the people who were interviewed. The central section of the article discusses who was interviewed and differing reactions from school boards and suburban and urban parents and teachers. The concluding section raises questions for additional investigation.

3. *Consider the text in a rhetorical context—figure out the nature of the conversation.*

    This report attempts to find out various stakeholders' attitudes about a proposed change in high school starting time. There is obviously an assumption that attitudes will vary, and the article attempts to present a preliminary report on these attitudes and suggest areas for further research. The author presents a balanced perspective; her textual "self" is that of a researcher who is interested in pursuing questions related to the topic.

4. *Situate the text within the discipline.*

This text was written by a legitimate academic organization whose purpose is to present information as objectively as possible. If you were working in an area related to this topic, you may want to use this article as a springboard to justify your research.

5. *Identify areas of intertextuality.*

The article refers to previous studies of this topic, both of which are accessible online. You may wish to read these studies as well. However, because both of them were written by the same person, you may want to find other studies on this topic.

6. *Compare this text to other texts you have read.*

You may compare this text with research that suggests that adolescents tend to sleep later in the day and perform better when they have had sufficient sleep.

7. *Ask why you are reading this text.*

You may be reading it to justify further research on this topic; there are a number of suggestions at the end.

8. *Create signposts in the text.*

Keywords of interest in this article refer to the different groups or stakeholders involved in this controversy, and you may flag these within the text. If you were looking for a thesis/dissertation topic, you may highlight these terms and circle the issues at the end that point to additional research questions.

9. *Keep track of your own location.*

As you read, you may consider how the study described in this report furthers your own progress. Did it point you in a direction worth pursuing? Does it build on previous work?

10. *Evaluate your presence in the text.*

This is a short article and probably does not require rereading. But perhaps you may make a note of the groups that were studied, with the idea that you may revisit this section.

Applying Strategies for Mapping a Text

Following are some suggestions for further applying the strategies discussed in this chapter:

1. Find a seminal article in your discipline, perhaps one you have been assigned for class, and apply as many of the strategies discussed previously as you think are worthwhile. Can you situate that article in terms of the writer's goal or motive? Does the writer address a controversy or problem in the discipline? Is there a conversation that he or she is joining? Can you point to a statement in the text that enables the author to enter the scholarly conversation?

2. Find an article in your field, perhaps one you have been assigned for class, and analyze the "moves" it uses to introduce the topic to the reader. Consider the extent to which you can use these "moves" in your own writing.

3. In an article published in *Composition Forum,* Carra Leah Hood addresses an issue in the field of rhetoric and composition. Read the excerpt from that article here and construct a "map" of that text, noting, in particular, the "sea of intertextuality." Using a topic that is related to your thesis or dissertation, analyze and imitate the "moves" in this text.

Lying in Writing or the Vicissitudes of Testimony

By Carra Leah Hood

In "Requiring Students to Write About Their Personal Lives," which appeared in the 17 February 1993 issue of the *Chronicle of Higher Education,* Susan Swartzlander, Diana Pace, and Virginia Lee Stamler note the contradiction between the "shockingly unprofessional" practice of asking students to write about their personal traumas in writing courses and the common occurrence of such assignments (B1). They argue that this practice remains common because the debates about whether or not "personal writing helps students to develop the necessary academic skills" ignore the ethical concerns of requiring students' self-disclosures in writing for school (B1). Most importantly, the authors point to ethical concerns with grading, retraumatization, and gender. It is their contention that attention to these concerns will convince a professor inclined to ask students to write about their personal traumas not to do so. For instance, any professor who may argue that "having students write on what they care about most and know best is the only way to get them to write well" would reconsider an assignment that could potentially retraumatize the student writer (B1). A male professor may change his assignment after being apprised of the gender concerns such disclosures present to female students, the authors predict.

In 2001, Jeffrey Berman published *Risky Writing: Self-Disclosure and Self-Transformation in the Classroom,* his contribution to the debate about the value of students' self-disclosure in their writing courses. In this study, Berman argues that student writing about trauma leads to educational, aesthetic, and therapeutic achievements. His position highlights, first of all, at least one instance of a writing teacher dismissing the ethical concerns raised by Swartzlander, Pace, and Stamler. Secondly, Berman's analysis demonstrates superficial understanding of the relationship between writing, trauma, and recovery, a superficiality that is all too common in the debates about the appropriateness or inappropriateness of requiring students' self-disclosures in their writing courses.

In an effort to restate the ethical issues embedded in essay assignments that ask students to explore traumas in their life, this essay conceptualizes the place of writing, and language use more generally, in recovery as much more complicated, much less controlled, much more diffuse, and much less significantly associated with particular writing assignments in school than Berman and even Swartzlander, Pace, and Stamler assume.

Hood, Carah Leah. "Lying in Writing or the Vicissitudes of Testimony." *Composition Forum* Issue 14.2, Fall 2005. Reprinted with permission.

4. Read the three paragraphs reprinted here from an article by Edward G. Goetz, "Desegregation Lawsuits and Public Housing Dispersal." This article examines the effects of one desegregation lawsuit, "*Hollman* v. *Cisneros* in Minneapolis." Which mapping strategies can you use to understand and evaluate this text?

Desegregation Lawsuits and Public Housing Dispersal

By Edward G. Goetz. Journal of the American Planning Association *70, 3, Summer 2004.*

In the past two decades, the U.S. department of Housing and Urban Development (HUD) has settled a series of lawsuits across the country related to the segregation and spatial concentration of public housing units. These lawsuits were typically filed as housing discrimination cases in which it is alleged that the local housing authority and HUD willfully and negligently segregated subsidized housing projects in a predominantly minority neighborhoods. Since the late 1980s, HUD has entered into consent decrees in more than a dozen of these cases nationwide. Although the settlements differ in detail from case to case, there are several common themes that run through them all. Typically, the settlements call for the demolition of public housing, the construction of replacement housing on scattered sites, and the development of a "housing mobility" program to facilitate desegregative moves by low-income public housing families (Popkin, Galster, et al., 200a). In addition, several of the settlements call for the merging of Section 8 and public housing waiting lists, along with community development in areas surrounding the public housing sites.

The combination of public housing demolition, redevelopment, and housing mobility programs makes these legal settlements hybrids of two federal programs, HOPE VI Public Housing Redevelopment (HOPE VI) and Moving To Opportunity (MTO). The settlements deal with older public housing much as the HOPE VI program does—by emphasizing demolition and redevelopment of the sites into lower density, mixed-use developments. Many of the consent decree sites have, in fact, made use of HOPE VI program funds to accomplish those objectives. In addition, however, the lawsuits incorporate the MTO model of geographically restricted housing vouchers and mobility counseling to facilitate the deconcentration of poor households.

In this article, I summarize the implementation of the consent decree in one of these lawsuits, *Hollman* v. *Cisneros* in Minneapolis, and investigate the degree to which the decree has resulted in the dispersal and deconcentration of subsidized families. The Hollman settlement is an appropriate exemplar for these lawsuits because it incorporates virtually all of the elements that are included in any one of them.

Reprinted with permission.

Works Cited

Bazerman, Charles. "Intertextuality: How Texts Rely on Other Texts." *What Writing Does and How It Does It.* Charles Bazerman and Paul Prior, Eds. New Jersey: Lawrence Erlbaum, 2004. 83–96.

Bhatia, Vijay K. Analysing Genre: Language Use in Professional Settings. London: Longman, 1993–97.

Greene, Stuart. "Exploring the Relationship Between Authorship and Reading." *Hearing Ourselves Think: Cognitive Research in the College Classroom.* New York: Oxford UP, 1993. 33–51.

Swales, John. *Genre Analysis: English in Academic and Research Settings.* Cambridge: Cambridge UP, 1990.

5

———————————

Writing and Revising

> Words words words words words
> Look scholarly on page but
> Do I have a point?
>
> —Kathy Leslie

YOUR PROPOSAL HAS been approved. You have done your research, and you have read many articles and books concerning your topic. Your notes and materials are organized into computer folders and/or in actual folders; they are filed neatly or perhaps piled on your desk, shelves, or floor. You have done your homework. Now it is time to write a first draft.

Easier said than done? Yes, indeed. Anxiety-provoking? Certainly. *Beginning* to write a thesis/dissertation (also articles, books, papers for class, reports, and so on) is often stressful even for writers who have a clear idea about what they want to say. In fact, a temptation for graduate students is to continue reading and engaging in more research as a way to avoid actually writing. The task can seem overwhelming. Where is the best place to start? What sort of organizational structure is most effective? How can coherence be maintained throughout such a long work?

The good news is that you can always revise. *Good* writing is *revised* writing, a statement that pertains particularly to the writing of a long and important work such as a thesis/dissertation (notice that at the end of the first paragraph, I used the words "first draft"). All texts, even relatively short ones, develop and change as the writing proceeds, and a thesis/dissertation is even more likely to evolve as you become more deeply immersed in your topic. As you proceed, you may decide to read additional articles, modify your research strategy, or discard some of what you have. Whatever you write likely will need revision—maybe several revisions—of each individual chapter and of the thesis/dissertation as a whole. So don't worry about getting everything right the first time. Find a place to begin and then get started writing. Even if you absolutely *hate* what you have written and cringe at the thought of anyone reading it, you can always revise. But you can't revise if you haven't written anything.

This chapter discusses strategies that can help you develop and revise a draft, based on the genre and process approach that informs this book as a whole. It focuses on activities that will help you get started on a first draft and suggest strategies for what I refer to as "global revision"—revision that focuses on main ideas and structure instead of sentence-level grammar and style, which are covered in Chapter 9, "Working with Grammar and Style."

Genre Expectations of the Thesis/Dissertation

Because you have been doing so much reading and research and have focused on each component of your topic, you may have lost sight of the genre requirements of the end product you are creating. A simple way to begin writing the first draft, then, is to review the requirements of this genre, focusing in particular on the following characteristics (these were discussed in more detail in the Introduction, "Writing a Thesis or Dissertation: An Overview of the Process") and in Chapter 1, "Getting Started":

- A thesis/dissertation identifies a problem or issue that is well defined and worth addressing. The problem or issue leads to the posing of a research question and a consideration of how it might be answered.

- A thesis/dissertation is a persuasive scholarly document that presents an *argument* and supports it with evidence. Its goal is to convince a committee and other members of the academic community of the following:
  - The problem, situation, or issue is significant to the profession.
  - The problem, situation, or issue has not been treated adequately in previous scholarly work (although it may have been addressed previously in some way).
  - The author has created or discovered a credible strategy or direction for addressing the problem, situation, or issue.

As you review these genre requirements, think about where you would like to begin writing about the "problem" you will be discussing. Then begin by *using material that you have already written in your thesis/dissertation proposal*. Chances are, you already have sections that define the problem and review the literature. Can you transfer this information into an introductory chapter? *Transferring material you have already written* is an excellent way to begin a writing project because you can develop it, move it around, or discover new directions to explore. It is reassuring to see text on a page, so use the text you already have and proceed from there.

Create a Preliminary Template

To help you begin to write, a good idea is to create a "preliminary template." This requires the following activities:

- Selecting a provisional model
- Developing a tentative table of contents
- Restating the overall purpose of your thesis/dissertation

Selecting a Provisional Model

In Chapter 1, I recommended that you examine theses/dissertations online or in your university library, to become familiar with possible topics or directions you might develop. Now that you have chosen a topic and have written your proposal, it will be useful for you to look at other theses/dissertations again, this time paying particular attention to their form and structure. The thesis/dissertation is a particular genre; to write successfully in that genre, you have to understand it thoroughly—in essence, to get inside of it and obtain a sense of what it is supposed to be in terms of focus, development, and structure. To gain this insight, examine several that were written recently in your department and consider the following questions:

- Where is the main point of the thesis/dissertation usually presented?
- How many chapters do they usually have?
- How long is a typical chapter?
- Is there a separate chapter for the "Review of the Literature," or is it included within an introductory chapter?
- What sort of information is contained in the conclusion?

Examine several theses/dissertations in the context of these questions. Then select a provisional model that you can use to construct a "template" for your own work. This template is only "preliminary" because you likely will modify it as your writing proceeds. But in the initial phase of writing a first draft, the preliminary template will help you define your project and separate it into manageable sections. The template can thus serve as a plan or set of directions.

Constructing a Tentative Table of Contents

An important component of the preliminary template is a tentative table of contents, and you may be wondering how you can do this before you have written anything. Remember that the key word here is *"tentative"* and that you have already done a lot of work investigating this topic and organizing your work in folders. These folders can serve as the basis for your tentative table of contents. In fact, because you have done so much reading and research in the process of formulating your topic, you likely will probably have more folders than the number of chapters you need. As you look through your notes, you may find that you have collected so much material and have considered so many possible directions for each chapter that you don't know which one to pursue. As my colleague Julie Neff Lippman points out...

> Graduate students often have too much material rather than not enough, and they are often overwhelmed by the amount of it. The abundance of material leads to writer's block or problems with focus. They hate to leave anything out.

The feeling of being "overwhelmed" by research notes is understandable, as is the desire not to "waste" anything. After all, you have explored so many potential subareas of your topic and have done so much work. Shouldn't you try to use everything?

My recommendation is to use what you can initially without worrying about what is left over. Mark the notes you can use initially in your first draft and don't concern yourself with what you are omitting. As you write, you may decide to include some of the material that you didn't think you could use at first. Some of it you might decide to use in a later revision. But some material you may have to save for a different project later, and you shouldn't worry about that. My experience tells me that most work does not go to waste, even if it is not used in the original project for which it was intended. Often an unforeseen project several years later may call for a topic you had investigated for your thesis/dissertation but weren't able to use. Begin writing a first draft by using what you can, add material as the need arises, and keep the rest for another day.

Recalling the Overall Purpose of the Thesis/Dissertation

Constructing a preliminary thesis/dissertation template and using the folders you have created to construct a tentative table of contents will help you get started writing each chapter. However, sometimes students become so involved in the unity of each chapter that they lose sight of the big picture—the thesis/dissertation as a whole. This is a very common problem in the writing of a long and complex work; it is one that I experienced myself. When I wrote my first draft, I focused on each chapter on its own, as if it were a separate seminar paper. Then when I had completed every chapter, I discovered that although each chapter was well organized, I hadn't developed an overall theme or thesis that connected them to the dissertation as a whole; nor was it apparent how one chapter connected with another. The explanation for this problem was simple: I didn't have an overall theme when I began, and only when I had written my first draft did I discover one. In a subsequent revision, I began to get a sense of the "big picture" so that in a later revision, I was able to link each chapter to the main idea I was trying to develop.

To keep focused on your overall goal, I suggest that you open a new window on your computer in which you list the following information:

- My tentative title is _____.
- My topic is _____.
- The problem or question I plan to address is _____.
- My main argument is _____.
- The method or approach I plan to use is _____.
- The relationship of *this* chapter to my main argument is _____.

Of course, if you are working on a small screen or away from a computer, you can write this information on a sheet of paper. Wherever you write them, it is useful to review these questions frequently as a means of sticking to your overall purpose and not getting lost in each individual chapter. Think of each chapter as a step along a path to developing a main idea for the thesis/dissertation as a whole, and use keywords along that path to remind the reader of that main idea.

The following shows an example of how a thesis/dissertation template can be used. It is based on an M.A. thesis written by Christina Saidy in the field of rhetoric/composition. I have italicized keywords that refer to its overall purpose.

Title: *Mind the Gap: Envisioning a Secondary University Writing Continuum*

1. My topic is *the gap in scholarship regarding secondary and university composing processes.*

2. The problem or question I plan to address is *why there is such a gap.*

3. My main argument is *that the discipline of composition has focused only on the teaching of writing at the post-secondary level, both theoretically and pedagogically. This discrepancy can be seen in the textbooks intended for high school teachers as opposed to college teachers.*

4. The method or approach I plan to use is a *rhetorical analysis of textbooks intended for both levels.*

- Chapter 1: "History and Hierarchies in *Composition*"
  This chapter discusses the establishment of Composition as a discipline. It shows that *the gap between university and secondary writing* has been perpetuated by the emphasis of this discipline.

- Chapter 2: "Texts for University Instructors"
  This chapter discusses texts for university writing instructors and the way *these texts narrow their audiences to a primarily university-level audience.*

- Chapter 3: "Texts for Secondary Instructors"
  This chapter explores *texts* for secondary writing instructors, focusing on the ways that *these texts are only covertly theoretical, if at all.*

- Chapter 4: "Shaping Secondary Teachers"
  This chapter evaluates syllabi for methods courses, to explore the ways that *secondary teachers are—or are not—trained as teachers of writing.*
- Chapter 5: "Widening the Gap: Common Practices in Secondary Schools"
  This chapter shows how current secondary writing practices serve to broaden the *gap between secondary and university writing.*
- Chapter 6: "Bridging the Gap: Writing as a Continuous Process"
  This chapter introduces *suggestions for narrowing the gap between secondary and university writing.*

Note in this template how each chapter refers back to the overall goal of the thesis through the use of keywords. As you construct your template and begin to write each chapter, make a list of words you consider to be "key." Look for those words particularly in the beginnings and endings of each of your chapters. They are the "glue" that keeps each chapter connected to your thesis/dissertation and to one another.

You can use to create a preliminary template for writing and revising your thesis/dissertation:

Preliminary Template

Provisional model:
This is based on (a model, department form, etc.)

Main features of this model:
Tentative Table of Contents (For each chapter, write a sentence summarizing the content you plan to include.)

Introduction

Chapter 1: Title, Summary

Chapter 2: Title, Summary

Etc.

Restatement of Overall Purpose of Thesis/Dissertation

You might find that the process of developing a preliminary template raises questions in your mind about your overall purpose. As you proceed, you will delve more deeply into your topic, and you may become aware of new ideas through continued reading or participation in conferences and list serve discussions. Continuous involvement in your topic is, of course, stimulating and interesting. However, you need to weigh the benefits of including a new direction or idea against that of finishing your degree. When you want to add new material or change a direction, I suggest that you check with your advisor, particularly if the change will involve a great deal of additional time.

The Revision Process

As I emphasized at the beginning of this chapter, revision is essential to the task of writing a thesis/dissertation, whether you submit each chapter to your advisor as you write it or you wait until you have written a complete first draft. Of course, you should consult your advisor about how he or she wants to receive your work because advisors vary in their preferences. My own preference is for graduate students to submit each chapter as they write it because I can then help them become aware of potentially problematic tendencies or misunderstandings before they proceed further.

What is the best way to revise? Of course, there is no one answer to this question. If you have developed a writing process that works well for you, by all means, continue to use it. There is no one "right" way to compose, whether you are writing a thesis, a dissertation, or a novel. Some writers revise as they write, rethinking and editing while they complete a first draft. Others finish a draft, put it aside for a while, and then revise it. Many do both revising and editing while writing a first draft and then revising again after the draft is finished. A distinguished scholar I know uses a voice-recognition program to dictate as many ideas as possible, and they all tumble onto the page in no apparent order. He then reviews those ideas, constructs an organizational structure, and revises it until he is satisfied.

Global Versus Surface Revision

In thinking about revision, it is useful to distinguish between *global revision* and *surface "editing."* Global revision involves serious conceptual and organizational rethinking and can result in significant alteration in the purpose, thesis, structure, and overall main point. It means what the word *"revision"* implies—a *re*vision or *re*seeing of the purpose, structure, and overall point. It is different from surface editing, which involves correcting spelling, grammar, and style; in general, it is probably more efficient to focus on global revision before editing or making stylistic changes. After all, why edit sentences that may not remain in the thesis/dissertation in a final draft? Also writers who focus too heavily on surface elements can remain "stuck" on one particular word or sentence for quite some time.

Nevertheless, some writers feel compelled to tinker with sentence structure and style even when they are aware that the entire direction and organization may change. These writers can't seem to move away from an awkward section, sentence, or word until they have attempted to correct it. For those writers, the activity of wrangling with the surface of a text seems, paradoxically, to help them reconsider additional ideas and develop a new perspective.

Consider what works well for you and think about how you can apply the writing process you have developed as a graduate student to the writing of your thesis/dissertation. These additional questions will enable you to gain insight into your habits as a writer:

Writerly habits:

- How many drafts do you usually write for one paper?
- How much do you write before you read over what you have written? A sentence? A paragraph? The whole paper?
- Do you change things in your writing as you go along? Or do you write a whole draft without stopping?
- Do you show your drafts of papers to anyone?
- What is your usual reaction to early drafts of your paper?
- When you finish a draft, do you ever put it away for a while before you read it?
- Have you ever thrown away an entire draft of a paper and started over again?

Look over your responses to these questions. What has worked best for you in the past? What aspects of your work usually need the most revision? On the basis of these responses, can you construct a plan for revising your work?

Global Revision

Whereas surface revision or "editing" focuses on sentences, words, and style, global revision means thinking about changing a text in a substantive way and includes the following goals, which pertain particularly to the writing of a thesis/dissertation:

- To find a focus in a lot of material
- To reorganize
- To refocus a main point
- To add support

- To decide whether additional research is needed

How can you accomplish these goals? Here are some suggestions:

- Read the chapter aloud.
- Read the chapter many times, leaving time between readings.
- See if you can locate the chapter's main point or thesis statement.
- Look for keywords that pertain to the overall focus of the chapter and to the thesis/dissertation as a whole.
- Look for the strengths in the chapter.
- Look for inconsistencies in the chapter.

Revising for Organization and Structure

The Structure of Each Chapter

Although each chapter is a component of the thesis/dissertation as a whole, each one should have its own focus and an organizational structure that helps develop that focus. After you have written a draft of a chapter, create an outline of its major points, noting gaps in sequence or logic. Are your ideas presented in a logical sequence? Or should you change the order in which they are presented? Which idea should you present first?

An important point to keep in mind when revising for organization and structure is that the organization scheme you are using should be apparent to your reader. At the beginning of each chapter, provide a brief overview of how you plan to structure your ideas. Include sentences that show this plan such as

This chapter discusses _____, focusing on _____.

Examine the models you have selected to note how each chapter is organized. How does the writer make that organizational scheme apparent to the reader? Are there structures you can adapt for your own work? If you are working in a writing group, you might ask a member to read at least the beginning of each chapter, to see if he or she can predict the organizational pattern you have constructed.

Students often ask if there is there a particular scheme that is regarded as most effective for presenting ideas. My response is usually either "No" or "It depends on what you are trying to accomplish." In deciding what sort of idea structure to present in a chapter, recall that each one aims to further your argument or main point in some way. Sometimes it is effective to build up to your most important idea as the chapter proceeds. On the other hand, busy readers usually pay most attention to points presented at the *beginning* rather than at the end of a text. Therefore, assuming that both your advisor and the members of your committee are likely to be busy people, it is reasonable to present your most significant point first, when their attention is most concentrated. Then discuss your major points in descending order of importance. Of course, it is also important to remind your reader of how each point connects to the theme of the chapter and to the thesis/dissertation as a whole.

Using a Function Outline

A useful way to ensure that each chapter is well structured is to analyze it using a "function outline." A function outline consists of brief statements about how each section functions within the chapter, in terms of its relationship either to the main point of the chapter or to one of its supporting points. The main purpose of the function outline is to help a writer see where the structure of a text may need additional work and to initiate revision. You can use the following function outline worksheet to examine the structure of each of your chapters.

Function Outline Worksheet

A function outline consists of brief statements about how each section within a chapter functions in relation either to its main point or to one of its supporting points. The purpose of writing a function outline is to focus attention on the structure and coherence of the chapter and to initiate revision.

Steps for Writing a Function Outline

1. State the overall purpose or main point of the chapter.

   Main Point or Overall Purpose in the Chapter: _____

   _____

2. Skim the chapter, highlighting the main supporting ideas. Briefly summarize those ideas:

   First Main Point _____

   Second Main Point _____

   Third Main Point _____

   Fourth Main Point _____

   Fifth Main Point _____

   Sixth Main Point _____

3. Go through the chapter paragraph by paragraph, noting how each one functions to support main or supporting points. As you read, think about the following questions: Does the paragraph develop a main point? Does it provide background material? Is it an example? Does it present a counterargument? Find keywords in the paragraph that refer back to the main purpose of the chapter and to the overall theme of the thesis/dissertation.

4. Having examined every section of your chapter in terms of function, note which ones need modification or elaboration. Do you need explanatory sentences or additional evidence to support your main ideas?

Signposting the Organization of Your Ideas

No matter what order of presentation you decide on, your essay will not hold together unless you link each point to your main thesis by through signposts or "cueing devices." Signposts remind your reader of how each point supports the main point of the essay, review where the essay has been, indicate where it is going, and keep the reader from getting lost. Most readers can focus on only a limited amount of information at any one time; therefore, signposts or cueing devices help readers understand how the essay is structured so they will not become confused.

The simplest method of signposting is to say simply, "This is my first point; this is my second; etc." More subtle signposts do not announce their presence so obviously, but instead smooth the transition between ideas. Signposting can be achieved through transitional words and phrases such as *however, nonetheless, therefore, moreover, additionally, nevertheless,* and many others. These are some transitional devices that are frequently used for signposting:

- To establish cause and effect: *therefore, thus, as a result, consequently*

- To show similarity: *similarly, in the same way*

- To show difference: *however, on the contrary, but, despite that*

- To elaborate: *moreover, furthermore, in addition, finally*

- To explain or present examples: *for example, for instance, such as, in particular*

Signposting can also be achieved through transitional paragraphs that act as a link between two ideas and prepare the reader for a new topic or indicate a forthcoming order of ideas. Here is an example of a transitional paragraph:

The fast food industry has been castigated by the media as the major cause of the obesity of today's adolescents. However, four additional causal factors must also be considered.

In this paragraph, the author refers to four issues, which one assumes will be explained further in subsequent paragraphs.

Revising by Considering Purpose and Audience

Revision of each chapter can also get started if you think about the possible reactions of an intended audience to the text you have written. When you wrote your thesis/dissertation proposal, you selected a few "text-partners, "the significant texts in your discipline toward which you could direct your own writing. Now use your text-partners to initiate revision by rereading them or at least looking over notes you may have written at an early stage of your research. Then try to imagine what the authors of these texts would likely say as they read your work. What questions might they have? Would they object to any of your arguments or conclusions? Would they expect you to include material that you might have omitted? In the context of the subtitle of this book, "Entering the Conversation," recall that writing often occurs not in isolation, but in a "room" in which a discussion is taking place. Re-enter that "room" as you think about revision, and listen to the "voices" of your "textpartners" as they converse about your topic and read what you have written so far. What revisions would they be likely to suggest? You can also show drafts of chapters to "real" partners—members of a thesis/dissertation writing group, for example.

Revision can also be stimulated by the process of "nutshelling," which, as its name implies, means to reduce an idea to its essence, rendering it tight enough that it can fit into a "nutshell. Nutshelling can help you focus on a main point, enabling you to discern where it might need to be revised. Reread each chapter, then, and see if you can state in a nutshell what you think is its overall purpose and summarize how that purpose has been supported. When you have clarified the purpose of the individual chapter, consider how the chapter helps develop the thesis/dissertation as a whole. Can you forge a tighter connection?

Facilitating the Revision Process

This is a summary of suggestions that can help with global revision:

1. *Leave sufficient time to revise.*

   Even if you revise as you compose, it is a good idea to allow at least some time between completing a draft and revising it. If you begin to revise your essay immediately, right after you have completed a first draft, you will probably not be able to view your work objectively and will consequently miss many areas that need improvement. This is the disadvantage of "last-minute jobs"—they don't enable a writer to acquire sufficient distance from the text. However, if you leave the chapter alone for a while (even an hour is better than nothing), you will return to it with fresh eyes, viewing it almost as if you were the audience instead of the writer, and you will be in a better position to notice where revision is needed.

2. *Examine the focus of each chapter by reading introductory paragraphs aloud.*

   A first draft frequently has problems with focus. It may contain a lot of information that refers to the topic, but it may lack a main point that is clearly and explicitly stated or it may be embedded in a paragraph where readers are unlikely to notice it. Sometimes a main direction in a first draft is too broad to be addressed adequately. To narrow or clarify your focus, read the first few paragraphs of each chapter aloud, paying particular attention to your main point or purpose. Then see if you can locate where your main point, purpose, or direction is stated explicitly.

3. *Check your essay for adequate support.*

Ensuring that you have included a clear statement is an important component of revision. However, it is also important to determine whether that statement has been given adequate support. In particular, pay attention to the following:

• *Credibility*

How have you established credibility?

Have you adequately cited authorities? Do they provide support, or have you simply quoted from outside material to fill in space?

• *Evidence*

Have you supported your main points with compelling evidence? Do you need additional evidence or examples?

Are statistics relevant to this topic? If so, have you spent sufficient time analyzing them?

• *Elaboration*

In writing a first or even a second draft, writers often leave out important information or give certain points only cursory attention, which means that the chapter may require additional explanations, details, or examples. Actually, in revising each chapter, you should *expect* that you would need to do at least some additional writing because in a first draft, you probably will have left out something.

4. *Check each paragraph for function and connection to the main point of the chapter.*

As you reread each chapter, write the main point of each paragraph in the margin. Then see if you can find words or sentences within that paragraph that refer directly to that main point. Often a chapter contains a number of good examples, but its relationship to the main point is not well established. Go through each chapter paragraph by paragraph, adding linking words or transitional sentences as needed.

5. *Note arrangement and structure.*

Examine the order of your paragraphs and consider the following questions:

- Do your paragraphs lead naturally into another?
- Does the conclusion wrap things up adequately?
- Would another arrangement be more effective?

6. *Read some of your work aloud, paragraph by paragraph, checking for sentence-level coherence, fluency, and correctness.*

Reading aloud is a useful strategy for all aspects of revision, but it is especially useful for detecting sentence-level problems and areas where the text does not read smoothly. In reading for coherence, fluency, and correctness, think about the following questions:

- Does one sentence lead naturally into another?
- Are the sentences too short? Can these sentences be combined?
- Is there a need for additional details?
- Are your sentences too long? Can these be divided?
- Have you checked for common mechanical errors such as subject-verb agreement, pronoun reference, and missing or extraneous commas?
- Have you used your spell-checker?

  I address sentence-level issues in more detail in Chapter 9, but it is a good idea for you to think about surface revision even as you revise for purpose and structure.

Finally, in thinking about revision, you should leave enough time to use whatever human resources you have available to you.

If there is a writing center at your university, make contact with a tutor or consultant as you proceed with your revision. A number of graduate students are non-native speakers of English, and if you are one of them, you may find it useful to have a native speaker read your work to obtain feedback about the structure in which you have presented your ideas, as well as about the tone, the level of formality, or the appropriateness of particular terms. The proper acknowledgment of sources is an important issue to consider, so as you revise, be alert as to whether you have included so much information from published works that it over-shadows your own ideas. And, of course, it is important to make sure that you have acknowledged all quoted material in order to avoid inadvertent plagiarism.

If you are working with a thesis/dissertation group, share your work with other members. Or let a friend read problematic sec-tions, indicating areas that may not be clear or that might need adjustment in some way. You don't always have to act on every recommendation you receive. But another student or a friend might notice something that you, as the writer, may have over-looked.

Revision can be tiring, but it is the key to good writing. So keep up your spirits, and *keep writing*. If you maintain momentum and leave sufficient time for revision, you are likely to complete the job.

6

Writing the Literature Review

The King brought the miller's daughter to a chamber that was piled high with straw and gave her a spinning wheel and a reel. "Now set to work," he said. "And if between tonight and tomorrow at dawn you have not spun this straw into gold, you must die."

—"Rumplestiltskin," *Grimm's Fairy Tales*

IN THE CHILDREN'S STORY "Rumplestiltskin," a greedy king locks a miller's daughter in a room filled to the ceiling with straw. The king tells her that she has one night to spin all the straw into gold and that if she fails in this task, she will be killed. In utter despair and in complete confusion about how or where to begin, the Miller's daughter cries and wails until the gnome Rumplestiltskin comes to her rescue and performs the task for her.

The plight of the Miller's daughter can be compared to the situation that confronts many graduate students when they attempt to write a literature review for a thesis or dissertation. In exploring and discovering a topic, they have found many sources from books, journals, theses, newspapers, and more. Piles of these materials are stacked all around, on desks, tables, and floor, and they have diligently read their way through most of them, taking copious notes—computers bulge with information and threaten to explode. But having found all this "stuff," students are at a loss about how to organize it for a literature review. Which ones should be included? How should the review be structured? How much information should be included? What is the role of a literature review in developing a thesis or dissertation?

This chapter discusses the literature review as a genre, focusing on its purpose within a thesis or dissertation and on its role in enabling the writer to enter the disciplinary conversation. It also suggests strategies for working with sources and taking notes, to avoid "source loss"—a situation in which a writer loses bits of information needed for accurate documentation.

The Literature Review and the Writer, Reader, Text Relationship

If you input the term "literature review" into an online search engine, you will find several definitions of its components, and you might want to do this to obtain a variety of perspectives. Whatever definitions you find, however, it is important to consider them in the context of the writer/reader/text relationship, which is the underlying concept of this book. For example, the University of California, Santa Cruz, defines the literature review as follows:

> [A] literature review surveys scholarly articles, books and other sources (e.g. dissertations, conference proceedings) relevant to a particular issue, area of research, or theory, providing a description, summary, and critical evaluation of each work. The purpose is to offer an overview of significant literature published on a topic.

This definition, although correct in many ways, does not discuss the literature review in terms of the interaction between the *writer* (you, the graduate student writing a thesis or dissertation), the intended *audience* (your thesis advisor and the scholarly community), and the *text* (the thesis or dissertation), which, as was discussed in Chapter 3, "The Proposal as an Argument: A Genre Approach to the Proposal," is a type of argument). In the context of writing a thesis or dissertation, then, I define the literature review in this way:

A Literature Review surveys scholarly articles, books, and other sources (e.g. dissertations, conference proceedings) relevant to a topic for a thesis or dissertation. Its purpose is to demonstrate that the *writer* has insightfully and critically surveyed relevant literature on his or her topic in order to convince an intended *audience* that this *topic* is worth addressing.

Defining the literature review in these terms is to understand it as a means of entering the scholarly conversation. For that purpose, the literature review, like the thesis or dissertation as a whole, can be viewed as a form of argument. Its goal is to demonstrate that you, the writer, have the necessary background to explore the topic you have chosen. By surveying existing literature critically and insightfully, you are justifying your choice for your intended audience and establishing the direction your thesis/dissertation will follow.

An Example of How a Literature Review Serves an Argumentative Purpose

In many theses and dissertations, the literature review is a chapter unto itself. However, due to limits of space, I cannot include in this book an entire literature review chapter from a thesis or dissertation to use as an example. What I can discuss, however, is an example from a published article, which often fulfills a similar function—to demonstrate that the writer is familiar with existing relevant literature, to justify the choice of topic, and thereby to enter the scholarly conversation.

A clearly written example of how a literature review fulfills an argumentative function is found in an article entitled "Teaching Genre to English First-Language Adults: A Study of the Laboratory Report," published in the May 2004 issue of *Research in the Teaching of English.* In that article, the authors, Carter, Ferzli, and Wiebe, address the question of whether written genres can be learned through explicit teaching or can only be acquired implicitly by writing within a discipline. Their article reports on research on teaching the genre of the laboratory report to first-language university students in biology labs. Their introduction, reprinted here, consists of a "Review of the Literature" that is used to justify their study. Read this review and write a one-sentence summary of each paragraph, focusing on what each paragraph *does*. You should also examine the organizational structure and note how the sources were summarized and referenced. Analyzing the structure of this introduction will give you a sense of how the literature review accomplishes its intended purpose. Although there is no "right" way to organize a literature review, examining a sample such as this suggests possibilities.

Title: "Teaching Genre to English First-Language Adults: A Study of the Laboratory Report"

Introduction

1. The persistent controversy attending the teaching of genre was brought to the fore by a set of articles published in RTE outlining opposing positions on the question of whether or not genre can be explicitly taught. Freedman (1993) argued that because genre knowledge is generally tacit and is acquired subconsciously in the contexts in which it is used, the explicit teaching of genres is not necessary, largely not possible, and perhaps even harmful. Williams and Colomb (1993) and Fahnestock (1993) countered Freedman's argument by pointing out that it is not always the case that context must precede and therefore determine the social forms of language for the context. They conclude that generic conventions can, therefore, be explicitly taught outside the contexts in which the conventions are applied. This exchange, however, has by no means put the matter to rest (e.g., Freedman 1999; Christie, 1999).

2. The issue is made more complex in that there are three schools of thought concerning genre, each with its own set of assumptions about teaching genre (Hyon, 1996; see also Paltridge, 2001). English for specific purposes (ESP)

is founded on the linguistic theories of John Swales (1986, 1990), particularly the application of structural move analysis, to describe broad organizational patterns in various genres for the instruction of adult nonnative speakers in academic and professional genres (Flowerdew, J., 1993; Henry & Roseberry, 2001; Salager-Meyer, 1990; Swales, 1981). Though the primary emphasis of this approach has been more on the analysis of genre rather than on the development of teaching strategies (Hyon, 1996), the grounding assumption is that genre can be explicitly taught (Bhatia, 1993; Flowerdew, L., 2000; Paltridge, 2001; Swales & Feak, 1994).

3. A somewhat similar position may be found in the Australian school of genre studies, based on the application of Michael Halliday's (1978; Halliday & Hassan, 1989) systemic functional linguistics to teaching primary and secondary students, with particular emphasis on those who are nonnative speakers and/or economically disadvantaged (Callaghan, Knapp & Noble, 1993; Christie, 1992; Martin, 2000). This approach to genre offers well-designed pedagogies for explicitly teaching genre (Christie, 1989; Martin, 1989), in accord with arguments that genre can be explicitly learned (Christie, 1999; Hammond, 1987).

4. A third approach to genre, New Rhetorical or North American, traces its origins to Carolyn R. Miller's (1984) understanding of genre as social action, a typified response to an often-repeated social situation. Scholarship in this area has been largely focused on ethnographic studies of generic contexts and the ways those contexts define and are defined by generic responses (Bazerman, 1988; Blakeslee, 1997; Devitt, 1991; Forman & Rymer, 1999). Because of their emphasis on generic contexts, advocates of the New Rhetorical approach tend to be skeptical that genre can be explicitly taught, arguing instead that genre knowledge must be acquired organi-

cally through active participation in authentic generic contexts (Berkenkotter & Huckin, 1995; Blakeslee, 2001; Freedman, 1993, 1999; Freedman, Adam, & Smart, 1994).

5. One of the key difficulties in answering the question of whether or not genre can be taught is that, as a number of researchers (e.g., Freedman, 1993; Henry & Roseberry, 1998; Hyon, 1996; Swales, 1990) have noted, there is little experimental research supporting either of the opposing assumptions. Studies of mainly English first-language (L1) primary-school children offer mixed conclusions (Chapman, 1995; Donovan, 2001; Kamberelis, 1999; Reppen, 1995; Wollman-Bonilla, 2000). Nunan's (1992) large-scale assessment of the Australian Disadvantaged Schools Project showed that English second-language (L2) children in low socio-economic schools produced better writing with explicit teaching of genre than students without such teaching. Research focusing on English L2 adult students has suggested that explicit teaching of genre may have positive effects on reading (Hewings & Henderson, 1987; Hyon, 1995) and on writing (Mustafa, 1995; Henry & Roseberry, 1998), though it is difficult to draw strong conclusions from the latter pair of studies. Henry and Roseberry's (1998) well-designed study, a control-group (quasi-random, pre- and post-test) experiment, showed significant improvement in two of the three variables tested to evaluate explicit teaching of a genre (travel brochure). Interestingly enough, however, the variable that showed no significant difference was the linguistic moves associated with the genre, even though these moves provided the primary basis for instruction.

6. In addition to being inconclusive as a whole, these studies of English L1 and L2 primary-school students and English L2 adults shed little light on the question of teaching genre to English L1 adults. It is certainly difficult to extrapolate from children's learning to adult learning.

And, as Grabe and Kaplan (1996) point out, L1 adults possess an implicit knowledge of genres in their language that L2 adults may not, suggesting that the latter may be more receptive to explicit teaching of genres in their second languages. Moreover, we have not been able to find any control-group experiments of teaching genre to English L1 adults. Thus, the debate initiated by Freedman in 1993 remains unresolved largely due to the lack of experimental research.

7. The study presented here does not definitively resolve the issue, but it does suggest a narrowing of the debate. We report a control-group experiment in which web-based instructional materials were used to teach the genre of laboratory reports to adult students in university biology laboratories. The results of this experiment indicate that genre can be taught effectively to English L1 adults within certain parameters.

(Carter, Michael, Ferzli, Miriam, and Eric Wiebe. "Teaching Genre to English First-Language Adults: A Study of the Laboratory Report." *Research in the Teaching of English*, 38.4 [2004]: 395–419.)

This clearly structured introduction shows how a literature review functions within a thesis or dissertation. Here is my functional analysis of this introduction, which you can compare to your own:

The first paragraph in the introduction provides a historical overview of a controversy: whether or not genres can be taught explicitly (some scholars say "yes"; others say "no."). The authors refer to the scholars who engaged in this controversy in 1993, briefly summarizing their conflicting positions.

In paragraph 2, the authors note further complexity in this issue because of three schools of thought concerning genre, each with its own set of assumptions about whether it can be taught explicitly. They discuss the English for Specific Purposes approach in this paragraph and summarize the other two approaches in paragraphs 3 and 4.

In paragraph 5, the authors note a further difficulty in answering the overall research question: the fact that there is little experimental research on this topic. They then summarize the major studies involving L1 and L2 children and L2 adults (the *L* refers to "language"). Then, in paragraph 6, they note a further gap in the literature: the fact that there have been no studies attempting to teach genre to L1 adults.

These six paragraphs prepare for the seventh, in which the goals of the research study are presented. Essentially, this concluding paragraph states, "Because there is a need (which we have established in the first six paragraphs), we have conducted an experimental study, and here is what we have found."

Exercise 1: Find an article in your discipline and analyze a section in which relevant literature is reviewed. How does the review demonstrate the qualifications of the author(s)? How does it justify the choice of topic and serve as a means of entering the scholarly conversation?

Exercise 2: Find a thesis or dissertation on the topic you plan to address in your own work. How is it similar to and different from the review in the published article you found in Exercise 1?

Exercise 3: The literature review analyzed earlier is concerned with a conflict—whether or not genres can be explicitly taught. Is there a conflict of perspectives in the topic you plan to address? Can you use this conflict to justify your choice of topic?

Questions Associated with a Literature Review

In planning your review, you might ask yourself the following questions:

1. What is my central question or issue that the literature can help define?

2. What is already known about the topic?

3. Is the scope of the literature being reviewed wide or narrow enough?

4. Is there a conflict or debate in the literature?

5. What connections can be made between the texts being reviewed?

6. What sort of literature should be reviewed? Historical? Theoretical? Methodological? Quantitative? Qualitative?

7. What criteria should be used to evaluate the literature being reviewed?

8. How will reviewing the literature justify the topic I plan to investigate?

Key Terms Associated with a Literature Review

The function of a literature review can also be understood through several key terms that you might reflect on as you write:

- **Compare and contrast**—You might compare and contrast different authors' views on an issue.

- **Criticize**—You might criticize methodology or perspectives in previous work, thereby showing the importance of your own.

- **Highlight**—You might highlight gaps in existing research.

- **Show**—You might show how your study relates to previous literature and is superior in some way.

- **Identify**—You might identify a problem, conflict, debate, or gap in the literature.

- **Define**—You might define a research area in a new way.

- **Question**—You might question the results of previous work.

Writing the Literature Review

Expect to Write Several Drafts

When should you start to write a literature review? I suggest that you begin a preliminary review as soon as you have an idea for your thesis or dissertation topic because the act of writing will enable you to gain a deeper understanding of what you are reading. But because you will not be an expert in your field right at the beginning of your exploration, it may take several years before you thoroughly understand work that you read earlier in your career. You should therefore expect to rewrite the review later in your studies, when you have acquired a deeper insight into your topic and are in a position to evaluate what you have read. You may have to rewrite it several times.

A qualification to that statement is that in some disciplines, institutions, and countries, particularly in the United Kingdom, students begin to work on a dissertation topic right at the beginning of their graduate studies. If you are a graduate student in such a program, the process of writing a literature review will be necessarily shortened.

Discovering Structure

A literature review is a well-developed reasoned text. It is not a list that describes or summarizes one text after another, and it is usually not a good sign if you find yourself beginning each paragraph with the name of the author or title of the work. Determining an effective structure, however, can sometimes be a challenge. When students initially write a literature review, it sometimes resembles an annotated bibliography rather than a review—that is, it summarizes the information in each article or book but doesn't link it to the overall direction of the thesis/dissertation or connect it with other works on a similar topic. Often it is organized chronologically simply because chronological structure is easy to use. Students also might keep adding studies as they read them, without integrating them into the work as a whole.

Unless developments over time are significant to the topic you are investigating, a chronological approach may not suit your purpose, and a simple add-on approach is unlikely to have much structure at all. The best structure is the one that enables you to focus on the issues you are addressing and to highlight the findings in the literature. The literature review analyzed earlier began the discussion by noting a conflict in the literature, discussed different approaches to the topic as noted in the literature, and eventually highlighted a gap in existing research. In that review, the literature concerned with the conflict and the gap led to the statement of what the study was about.

Of course, this is not the only way to structure a literature review, and you may have to try different organizational schemes before you discover the one that best suits your needs. Rewriting the review can be frustrating, but it is usually necessary if you want it to fulfill its function effectively. The following is another example of a review from a published article, which uses a different pattern than the one analyzed earlier. In this article, "Ethnic Preferences and Ethic Perceptions in Multi-Ethnic Settings," the statement of purpose *precedes* the Literature Review, a conceptual structure that may be more appropriate to your discipline than the example from the "genre" article. Using this pattern, the author is saying, in essence: "This is what my article is about. And the literature I cite sets a context for that statement."

Title: "Ethnic Preferences and Ethic Perceptions in Multi-Ethnic Settings"

[B]ecause of the changing demographic context, race and ethnicity continue to dominate both social discourse and political behavior in United States society. America at the beginning of the 21st century is as dominated by concerns with race as it was in the era immediately before and after the civil rights years of the 1960s. But while 30 years ago the moral high ground was held by those who argued that American society as a whole must redress the past wrongs of slavery and discrimination, now, if there is a moral high ground, it is a contest battlefield with many and conflicting voices. In this context, how can we move forward to an understanding of what is, and should be, the role of race and ethnicity in an increasingly mixed and spatially diverse society? Should we welcome the "end of racism" and distinctions based on race (D'Souza, 1995), or should we enlarge and strengthen the role of the government in the continuing 40-year attempt to create an integrated society? There are important questions that can be debated within the context of ethnocentrism and the continuing evidence of strongly held own race residential preferences. This paper reviews the debate about the causes of continuing separation of racial and ethnic groups and links separation and ethnocentrism. The paper argues that ethnocentrism is a powerful and important force in creating the structure of the urban mosaic. To ignore this force is to downplay the role of preferences and to overplay the role of discrimination rather than emphasizing the complexity of racial and ethnic relations.

The Debate About Race and Residential Separation

There is an ongoing debate in the research literature about the reasons for the continuing separation of racial and ethnic groups in the United States. That debate has been especially contentious with respect to the relative roles of economics, preferences and discrimination as competing explanations for the segregation that continues in the large metropolitan areas of the United States (Clark, 1986, 1989; Farley, 1997; Galster, 1988, 1989; Zubrinsky and Bobo, 1996). The debate has been particularly polarized about the role of preferences and ethnocentrism and whether patterns of mobility reflect the expressed preferences for various combinations of ethnic neighbors (St. John, 1996). While there is evidence that racial discrimination and prejudice are still factors in everyday U.S. life (Yinger, 1995), there is also evidence that there have been real gains in race relations (Schuman, Steeh and Bob, 1985). Moreover, it is clear that the racism of the last decade of the 20th century is very different from the racism of the racial exclusion acts of the 1920s. Unfortunately, much of the language about race and racism harkens back to past positions of Black and White relationships, and says little about a changed ethnic mix. Current thinking seems still to be set in past debates about discriminatory behavior by Whites against African Americans and by extension to Whites and other ethnic groups. The debate has only tangentially addressed the important and increasingly powerful role of multicultural ethnocentrism and the complexity of racial and ethnic relationships amongst more than two ethnic or racial groups.

(Clark, William A.V. "Ethnic Preferences and Ethnic Perceptions in Multi-Ethnic Settings." *Urban Geography*, 2002, 23:3, 237–256.)

This article, then, begins by raising the question of why races and ethnicities tend to live separately from one another, a question which leads to a statement of purpose: to argue that ethnocentrism is a powerful and important force in creating the pattern of where people live. The literature review then follows, discussing the various scholarly debates on this topic.

Question: Examine several articles in your discipline. Then find an example of a thesis or dissertation that is similar to the one you plan to write. Is the pattern of reviewing the literature similar to the "genre" article or to the one on race and ethnicity? Does it use a different form altogether?

Taking Notes and Minimizing "Source Loss"

Chapter 4, "Mapping Texts: The Reading/Writing Connection," discussed strategies that foster critical or rhetorical reading. In this chapter, I apply them to the process of organizing and keeping track of materials for writing a literature review. The goal is to make your notes as useful as possible for you when you write and to enable you to avoid or at least minimize "source loss." Source loss occurs when you have referred to a particular source and perhaps included it in your literature review or elsewhere in your thesis or dissertation, but you didn't write down part or all of the bibliographical information you need. Sometimes the loss is minimal, a missing page number or an author's first initial. Still, you have to relocate the source and skim through it, looking for the referenced text. But sometimes students forget to write down anything about a source to which they want to refer. Then there is a big problem as students try to reconstruct what they were reading, in order to locate the missing source. Be as careful as possible when you take notes, even though the process seems unnecessarily time-consuming. The strategies suggested here can help. But, of course, if you have a system that works well for you, by all means, continue to use it. "Order," like "beauty," is sometimes in the eyes of the beholder. One of my colleagues has an office that is piled with books, papers, and boxes—to me it looks like a serious mess. But somehow he can always find what he is looking for. For him, the mess has an order that is imperceptible to everyone else.

A Two-Pass Approach to Examining Sources

A common mistake graduate students often make is that they try to read every word of every source that is remotely related to their topic. If you are one of these students, you will find that the reading process will never end because the process takes an inordinate amount of time, and there is always more to read. In writing a literature review, keep in mind that it is not intended to summarize every text that relates to your topic—only those that are considered most relevant and significant to the direction you are pursuing.

The two-pass approach to examining sources will enable you to evaluate the credibility of the articles and books you read so that you can decide whether to use them in your literature review. Here is an overview of the process:

The First Pass: Previewing the Text

During the first pass, try to obtain a quick overview of the text. Consider the context of the scholarly conversation, decide whether the text is addressing a controversy, and see if you can figure out the author's purpose. Look at clues that provide this information, such as the title, publication information, abstracts, introductions, headings, results, conclusions, and easily discernible strategies of organization. If the source is an article, look for statements of purpose on the first two pages. If the source is a book, examine the table of contents and chapter headings. Briefly skim the introduction and conclusion. See if you can write a predictive summary of what the main point or perspective of this source might be.

As the writer of a thesis or dissertation, it is important that you learn to preview texts so that you don't waste time reading material that you ultimately will not use.

The Second Pass: Interacting with the Text

During the second pass, attempt to interact with the text by engaging in a critical dialogue with it. Your goal is to determine how much of it to accept, determine its value, and decide whether you plan to include it in your literature review. Such interaction involves evaluating the credibility of the author, examining theoretical or methodological premises, probing for perhaps unstated underlying assumptions, and assessing the type of evidence or support that is used. Do you agree with the method or approach? Does the author seem biased? Can this source be linked to others that address a similar topic or direction?

During this second pass, you will be reading more carefully. But even so, don't attempt to read every sentence. See if you can focus on the central argument of the text and make some tentative predictions.

Keeping Track of Sources

It is difficult to keep track of everything one reads. I don't think I have ever written an article or book that didn't require me to go hunting for a lost page number or author's name somewhere.

So many texts! So many ideas! So many pieces of paper! How does one manage not to lose necessary information? Here are a few suggestions:

Number and List Sources on a Source List

My first suggestion is to number every source you read and keep a list of each one. This idea may seem like a lot of extra work in the beginning, but at the end, when you are writing your "Works Cited" or " References" section, you will be delighted that all the bibliographical information is listed so accurately, and you will be able to paste it in directly.

Here is an example of a source list:

Source List

1. Freedman, A. (1993). "Show and Tell? The Role of Explicit Teaching in Learning New Genres." *Research in the Teaching of English* 27, 222–51.
2. Devitt, A. J. (1997). "Genre as Language Standard." In Bishop, W., and H. Ostrom (Eds.), *Genre and Writing: Issues, Arguments, Alternatives.* Portsmouth, NH: Boynton/ Cook, 45–55.
3. Williams, J., & G. G. Colomb. (1993). "The Case for Explicit Teaching: Why What You Don't Know Won't Help You." *Research in the Teaching of English* 27(3), 252–264.

Of course, you can also construct a list without using numbers. But numbers can help you remember the order in which you read a particular source and are especially useful when you have several sources by the same author. For example, if I want to reference three sources by Freedman, numbering each one allows me to distinguish them, especially if they were written in the same year. In the previous example, I have written my sources using the APA documentation system, enabling me to paste each citation into my "References" section when I am ready to compile it. If I were working in a discipline that used MLA, I would write my list in that system. Another safeguard against source loss is to use the numbers as well as the name of the source when you refer to it in your literature review or elsewhere in your thesis or dissertation. In a reference to Devitt in a draft of a literature review, for example, I might write "#1 Devitt" and then the appropriate page number.

Do not underestimate how difficult it is to keep track of the many sources you will be reading. Even a highly organized person experiences source loss from time to time. The good news is that although the task of finding a missing source can be frustrating and time consuming, usually the source can be found.

Taking Notes

The sources you use for your literature review will consist of many different types of texts—books, articles, interviews, journals, online sources. Some of these texts may be your own property, such as books you have purchased, journals to which you subscribe, or articles you have photocopied. But, of course, you are unlikely to own *all* the books you use, and you probably have not photocopied *every* article you have read. So how do you take notes about these sources so that you can recall their major points easily and incorporate their ideas into your literature review?

For the texts they own, many students like to use a highlighter to call attention to significant ideas they want to remember. I suggest, however, that whether or not you own a text and whether or not you like to use a highlighter, you take *actual notes*—preferably on the computer. Highlighting may seem a quick way to focus attention on text you want to remember or include, but after you have read a great deal, you may have difficulty locating specific points or quotations when you begin to write your literature review. Highlighting may seem like a good way to save time, and, certainly, you can use your highlighter to focus attention on important sections of the text. But if you supplement the highlighting with actual notes, you will have an easier time when you begin to write your literature review.

Students often ask whether they should take many or a few notes, and, of course, it really depends on the particular source and the amount of detail you find valuable in it. In general, I suggest taking slightly more notes than you think you will need. Often when you begin reading, you may not be quite sure of your topic, and you may refocus your thesis later to include aspects you hadn't considered in the beginning. As you move along in your research, you might discover that you need those additional notes after all.

How should you record your notes? Some students, having been taught in school to use note cards, still prefer to use this method. Note cards are easy to sort and, because they provide only limited room for writing, they can aid students in breaking down a topic into manageable parts. If you are in the habit of using note cards and find them an effective method for recording information, by all means, continue to use them—or any other system you have constructed for yourself.

My own experience suggests, however, that taking notes usually requires more room than a note card provides and that part of the note-taking process includes jotting down ideas about how this note might be useful. I like to record these ideas as they occur to me, writing them down right next to the note. Therefore, I need more room for writing than a note card allows. In general, I recommend taking notes on the computer and then printing them. You can then place them in folders, organized either by author's last name or by subject. If you don't always have access to a computer, I suggest a notebook with detachable pages. Then you can file the notes appropriately.

You can use two types of sheets for taking notes, the Source Sheet, which is used for recording notes about a single source, and the Synthesis Sheet, which is used to organize information about one aspect of a topic and may include notes from several sources.

The Source Sheet
A Source Sheet is used to record notes about a *single source*. It includes a summary of the source and contains information

obtained from that particular source. A Source Note Sheet helps you record your notes easily, and you can also use it to prepare your bibliography because you can alphabetize these sheets. You can use your computer to prepare a form for this sheet if you decide to work directly at the computer. If you prefer to work in hard copy, you can create copies of this sheet and fasten them into a notebook.

The following is a sample of a Source Sheet. The topic concerns whether new genres can or should be taught explicitly.

Source Number:	1
Author(s):	Freedman, Aviva
Article or Chapter Title:	"'Do As I Say': The Relationship Between Teaching and Learning New Genres"
Book or Journal Title:	*Genre and the New Rhetoric*
Editors:	Aviva Freedman and Peter Medway
Publisher (if appropriate):	Taylor and Francis
Date and Place of Publication:	London, 1994
Pages:	191–210
Short Summary:	Presents two hypotheses about the explicit teaching of genre: the "Strong hypothesis" states that explicit teaching is not necessary, not possible, and not useful. The "Restricted hypothesis" states that, under certain conditions, explicit teaching may contribute to learning.

Page #	Note	Idea About Note
194	Defines explicit teaching as involving "explicit discussions, specifying the (formal) features of the genres and/or articulating underlying rules.... Typically, such teaching is also decontextualized...."	Use to contrast with the Williams perspective. Also to show the narrowness of the definition.

In listing an author's name, you should begin with the last name so that you can easily alphabetize the sheets to create your bibliography. Note that there is also a section for a brief summary of your source so that you can remember what its overall purpose was. This is particularly useful if you want to compare different points of view on an aspect of your topic. It also forces you to think about what the main purpose of a source actually is (in some articles, this can be difficult to do). Note also that there is a space allotted for writing down the page number, a very important piece of information.

In the section marked "Notes" on the Source Sheet, you can either paraphrase an idea you want to remember or write it down as an exact quote. If it is an exact quote, remember to put quotation marks around it so that you can document it properly when you write your review. Note also the section of the Source Sheet marked "Idea About Note." Under that column, you are essentially asking yourself the question, "What am I going to do with this note?" As you read, you will get ideas that you cannot pursue immediately, and you may not remember them if you don't write them down. You may think to yourself, "This would provide a good argument against that other article I read." So you might write "Compare with [name] article." Or you may think, "This is a good example of...." Use this space to jot down ideas as they occur to you.

The Note Synthesis Sheet

The Note Synthesis Sheet is useful for organizing notes around a particular aspect of a topic, enabling you to compare perspectives from several sources. It includes enough information from each source so that you can incorporate it into your review with relative ease.

Here is an example of how a Note Synthesis Sheet can be used to compare perspectives on the explicit teaching of genre:

Topic: The Explicit Teaching of Genre

Author	Page	Note	Reason for Using
Freedman, Aviva	194	Defines explicit teaching as involving "explicit discussions, specifying the (formal) features of the genres and/or articulating underlying rules.... Typically, such teaching is also decontextualized...."	Most resistant of genre theorists about whether genre can be taught explicitly
Fahnstock, Jean	266	Responds to Freedman's article on explicit teaching by questioning how explicit instruction and genre should be defined. Considers how craft, as opposed to knowledge, can be learned.	Compare with Freedman
Williams and Colomb	261	"Thus it seems to make sense to use explicit teaching to focus younger students on the prototypical features of genres and to teach those features, not as rule-bound necessities, but as 'default' instances among a range of choices."	Queries Freedman's definition of explicit teaching and refutes her article point by point

Writing the literature review is an important element in writing a thesis or dissertation, in that it helps focus your thinking about what you are trying to accomplish in the work as a whole and enables you to enter the scholarly conversation. Using some of the strategies discussed here will help you avoid the problems students often experience in writing the literature review, particularly these:

1. **They try to include every work they have read.** Although you may feel that the effort you expended in reading all these texts should justify their inclusion in the literature review, you should include only those that pertain directly to your topic and justify the approach you plan to develop in your thesis or dissertation.

2. **They write lists of works, summarizing each one without relating them to the overall focus of the thesis or dissertation.** This structure does not enable the literature review to fulfill its function—to justify the approach to the topic and develop a rationale for exploring it.

3. **They don't keep accurate notes and lose track of bibliographic information.** At the beginning stages of writing a thesis or dissertation, students are often so focused on finding and developing a topic that they scribble notes carelessly, lose pages, and then find themselves missing important information when they have to write their "Works Cited" or "References" pages. Then they have to go to the library and attempt to track down all the missing sources, going back over their writing to figure out which information came from each source. To minimize source loss, you might experiment with some of the strategies discussed in this chapter or develop one of your own.

If you are now at the point of beginning your literature review, you might also take another look at those in theses and dissertations that are related to your topic. Perhaps they will suggest possibilities for further reading, or they may adhere to an organizational pattern that would work well for you. And keep your momentum going. Rumplestiltskin may have finished the job in one night. But for most of us, creating order from a large pile of material usually takes a lot more time.

7

<hr />

Using Visual Materials

"*Both images and words on script, print or digital pages engage the eyes. When images and words appear together in one discursive space, they operate synergetically. In this sense, written verbal rhetoric is visual rhetoric.*"

—Maureen Daly Goggin, "Visual Rhetoric in Pens of Steel and Inks of Silk: Challenging the Great Visual/Verbal Divide."

ALTHOUGH MOST THESES and dissertations communicate primarily through language—words, sentences, and paragraphs—visual materials can be an important asset in developing and supporting your ideas, particularly if your subject is concerned with graphic or numerical data. Visual representations such as tables, charts, diagrams, graphs, or photographs can serve as *focal points,* as enabling you to emphasize and clarify particular details for your readers. Such focal points can have a profound impact on the persuasiveness of your work, so it is important for you to consider how you can use them to your best advantage. This chapter discusses ideas that will help you use visual materials and offers suggestions for including them in your thesis or dissertation.

Visual Materials in a Thesis or Dissertation

This chapter emphasizes these main points:

1. Visual materials communicate ideas.

2. Visual materials can serve as *focal points* to draw the attention of readers.

3. The process of developing visual materials can enable a writer to understand and present a topic in new ways.

4. A writer can obtain useful suggestions for using visual materials by looking at the articles and books published by "text-partners."

5. If a writer is unclear about what information should be displayed, it can be useful to sketch out a possible presentation on a piece of paper before working with sophisticated computer graphic programs.

6. Visual materials can serve as support for an argument.

7. Visual materials should be constructed as clearly as possible so that readers can understand them easily.

8. Visual materials should be carefully labeled.

9. Visual materials should be referred to in the text.

Connections Between Print and Visual Rhetoric

Considerable attention is now being paid to what is known as "visual rhetoric," a term that is used to describe how visual images, as opposed to aural or verbal messages, communicate. Those who study visual rhetoric note that representational images are becoming increasingly important in communicating ideas and that they wield considerable influence on the beliefs, attitudes, opinions, and sometimes actions of those who view them. We are all familiar with the use of images in advertising and other obviously persuasive texts. But even in scholarly texts, which claim to be completely objective and are based on careful research, visual materials can create a persuasive *presence,* significantly penetrating the consciousness of the reader. In fact, in some cases, the power of visual materials can surpass that of words. As Charles A. Hill notes, "The phenomenon of *presence* is inherently linked to visual perception. It has often been remarked that a picture of one starving child is more persuasively powerful than statistics citing the starvation of millions" (29). In writing your thesis or dissertation, you might find that including graphic material will greatly enhance your ability to present your ideas.

Finding Examples Through Your Text-Partners

Chapter 2, "So What? Discovering Possibilities," discusses the concept of text-partners, defined as the texts to which your thesis or dissertation is responding. Text-partners not only are useful for helping you generate ideas; they also model possible ways of using visual materials. Look for the articles and books written by your text-partners, noting how they use visual materials. Look at other articles and books as well and imitate the way in which visual materials are used.

The Function of Visual Materials

When you decide to include visual materials in your thesis or dissertation, it is important to consider what *function* you want them to fulfill—that is, what you want them to *do* and how you plan to *use* them to communicate with your reader. Will they provide a *reference* point that will help you develop an idea more clearly? Will they serve as an *example*? Will they enable you to make a *comparison or evaluation* of some sort? Will they enable you to *examine a result* more thoroughly so that you can draw a *conclusion*? Will they help you *emphasize* a particular idea? Visual materials are inherently rhetorical (that is, they have an impact on a reader or audience), and they can do what words do—exemplify, compare, contrast, illustrate, refer, emphasize, and so on. It is important, then, to use visual materials as deliberately and strategically as possible, not simply to show how much data you have managed to locate, to fill up space, or to enhance the appearance of a page. To focus your attention on the functionality of visual materials, I suggest that you complete these sentences when considering whether to include a graphic in your text:

> The purpose of this (chart, graph, diagram, picture, etc.) is _____.
>
> This graphic will enable me to present the following ideas more clearly: _____.

Images have power, and, as the writer of a thesis or dissertation, you will be able to decide how they can function most effectively. Keep in mind that anything that stands out from the text, such as a photograph, design, table, graph, or chart—even text that is set off in some way—is likely to capture a reader's attention. In fact, the tendency of most readers is to focus immediately on the image, sometimes skipping a verbal explanation entirely. Thus, if presentation of data is important to your thesis, it is important for you to construct your *focal points* carefully, considering them in the context of the ideas you want to develop. If you are unclear about the sort of graphic material you want to display, it is useful to sketch out a possible design *by hand* on a piece of paper. The act of sketching out possibilities will help you figure out what you want to say and the best means of saying it through graphic representation.

Constructing a Focal Point

As the term implies, a *focal point* focuses attention on a particular idea or concept. If your thesis or dissertation includes numerical data, visual materials are usually considered a requirement, helping both readers and writers. Readers will find a visual representation of statistical information easier to understand than if numbers are simply included as part of the text; they will be naturally drawn to it as they read. Writers will find a graphic presentation useful for organizing data and focusing ideas.

Let us consider a hypothetical situation. Suppose your thesis or dissertation is concerned in some way with the topic of cat and dog ownership in the United States and that you had accessed statistical information about this topic. In writing this chapter, I was able to locate information about this topic relatively easily on the Internet, although, of course, if I were seriously conducting research, I would want to search more deeply. For the sake of illustration, though, suppose you had found some information about cat and dog ownership presented in the form of two lists, one about dog ownership and the other about cat ownership. A list is usually easy to read. However, two lists might be more difficult because we tend to read from left to right, not up and down. Moreover, although the presentation in the two lists is straightforward, this method might not be the most useful visual strategy if your goal were to *emphasize* or *compare* some aspect of this information. For example, you might want to show how many people owned dogs compared to those who owned cats; if you wanted to display further comparative data, presenting two lists would require a reader to keep moving between them, making it difficult to note points of comparison. Note the following two lists in Table 7.1, which present a great deal of information about pet ownership, but not presented in a way that enables easy comparison.

To focus your readers' attention on similarities and differences between the two lists, a table comparing different aspects of the topic would be more effective. For example, Table 7.2 would enable a writer to note that there were fewer "owned" dogs in the United States than "owned" cats (65 million compared to 77.6 million), but that there were more dog households than cat households (40.6 million vs. 35.4 million). The table form would also enable a writer to note that whereas 26% of cat owners owned two or more cats, only 23% of dog owners owned two dogs, and only 12% owned three or more dogs. Table 7.2 illustrates the comparisons that could be made using this type of visual presentation.

Table 7.1—U.S. Pet Ownership Statistics

U.S. Pet Ownership Statistics

The following statistics were compiled from the *American Pet Products Manufacturers Association (APPMA) 2003-2004 National Pet Owners Survey.*

Dogs
- There are approximately 65 million owned dogs in the United States.
- Thirty-nine percent of U.S. households (or 40.6 million) own at least one dog.
- Most owners (65%) own one dog.
- Twenty-three percent of owners own two dogs.
- Twelve percent of owners own three or more dogs.
- On average, owners have almost two dogs (1.6).
- Slightly more male dogs are owned than female dogs.
- Eighteen percent of owned dogs were adopted from an animal shelter.
- On average, dog owners spent $263 on veterinary related expenses in th past 12 months.
- Seventy-two percent of owned dogs are spayed or neutered.

Cats
- There are approximately 77.6 million owned cats in the United States.
- Thirty-four percent of U.S. households (or 35.4 million) own at least one cat.
- One-half of cat-owning households (51%) own one cat; the remaining own two or more.
- On average, owners have two cats (2.2).
- Slightly more female cats are owned than male cats.
- Sixteen percent of owned cats were adopted from an animal shelter.
- Cat owners spent an average of $113 on veterinary related expenses in th past 12 months.
- Eighty-four percent of owned cats are spayed or neutered.

Reprinted with permission

Table 7.2—U.S. Pet Ownership Statistics

U.S. Pet Ownership Statistics

	DOGS		CATS	
	Number	Percentage	Number	Percentage
Number of Owned Animals in the U.S.	65 million		77.6 million	
Number of Households Owning at Least One	40.6 million	39%	35.4 million	34%
Number of Animals Per Owner				
At Least One Animal		65%		34%
Two (Dogs)		23%		
Two or More (Cats)				26%
Three or More (Dogs)		12%		
Average Number in Household	1.6 per house		2.2 per house	
Gender	More male		More female	
Adoption from Shelter		18%		16%
Yearly Veterinary Expenses	$273		$160	
Spayed or Neutered		72%		84%

You can create tables in the form of text, data, or both. A *text table* consists of a list of points and can sometimes be referred to simply as a list (the table at the beginning of this chapter that listed concepts associated with visual materials is an example), and a data table, of course, consists of numerical information. Data tables should be constructed to display the facts that you want to emphasize, and the goal is to make them as easy to read as possible.

Table 7.2 allows readers to understand comparative data more easily than from two lists. Moreover, an additional advantage of presenting information in a table is that the *process* of creating the table requires writers to grapple with the information more intensively, enabling them to understand it in new ways. Creating the table directs writers' attention toward the points they want to emphasize and helps them figure out which focal points they want to develop. It might also provide insights about the topic that they didn't have before, raise questions, and suggest directions they might want to explore further. For example, when I constructed the table comparing cat and dog ownership, I began to wonder why there were more owned cats than owned dogs, even though fewer households owned cats than owned dogs. I also wondered why owned dogs tended more frequently to be male while owned cats tended to be female. If this were a real topic that I was actually investigating, creating the table would have directed me toward areas for further exploration. If you have amassed a great deal of numerical data and are not sure how you can use it in your thesis or dissertation, I offer the following recommendation:

Construct a table.

The act of constructing the table, *in and of itself,* will give you ideas that you didn't have before, help you discover additional information that you might need, generate questions about what you want to say about your topic, and lead you to think about new ideas. I have always found that the act of constructing a table has led me in new directions, and I strongly recommend it as a means of discovery.

Examples of Visual Materials

A table is a useful way to present precise numerical data. But of course, numbers can be presented in many other ways, such as bar graphs, line graphs, and pie charts. This section contains simple examples of how these can be used.

Bar Graphs

A *bar graph* is a useful method for showing the relationship among different quantities or amounts. It is a less precise method of display than a table, but it can be extremely effective because it is usually easy to read. Table 7.3 is an example bar graph based on a hypothetical survey concerned with the favorite pets of students.

Table 7.3—Favorite Pets of Students

Dogs	Cats	Fish	Birds	Other
920	720	250	290	410

This information could be displayed in the bar graph in Figure 7.1, to allow a reader to see at a glance that dogs are the favorite.

This graph is concerned with the relationship between two variables: the number of students and the choice of pets. However, bar graphs can also explain comparative data that refer to more than two variables. Figure 7.2 displays comparative data concerning the number of heart attacks suffered by men at various ages compared to those suffered by women.

This bar graph enables a reader to note easily that men and women differ in the number of heart attacks suffered at different ages. It indicates that the frequency of heart attacks increases with age and that men tend to suffer heart attacks more frequently than women, but that as people age, gender differences become less significant. Note that the graph has a clear title, that the graph is numbered as "Figure 7.2," and that it includes information indicating how it should be read (the numbers are presented in terms of percentages, and the light bar refers to men, and the dark bar refers to women).

Figure 7.1—Favorite pets of students

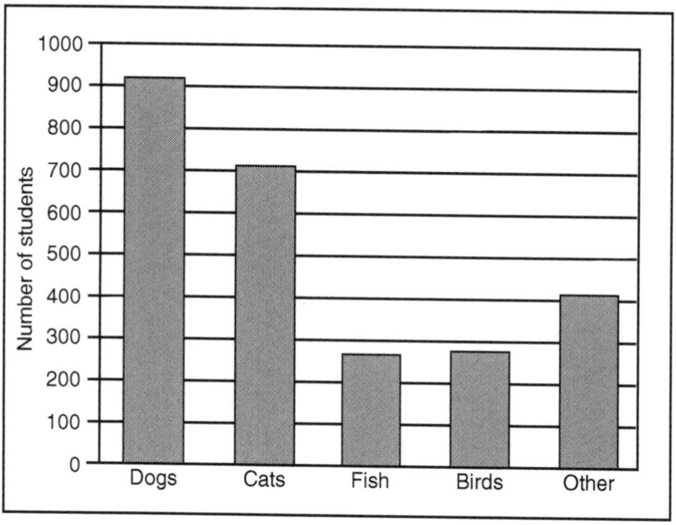

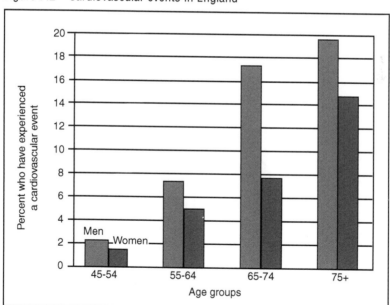

Source: Fictitious data, original graph.

Figure 7.2—Cardiovascular events in England

Source: Diagram constructed by author with data from Department of Health, Health Survey for England 2003. The Stationary Office: London.

The two bar graphs exemplify several formatting requirements for including graphic materials in your thesis or dissertation:

1. Each visual representation should be numbered, as in "Table 1," "Table 2," "Figure 1," "Figure 2," and so on.

2. Each visual representation should have a title that clearly indicates its purpose.

3. Each visual representation should include a key or legend that indicates how it should be read.

Figure 7.2 focused on differences between two groups: men and women. However, a bar graph can also show several variables, as in Figure 7.3, which is concerned with the immigrant professional workforce in selected states.

Figure 7.3—The immigrant professional workforce in selected states

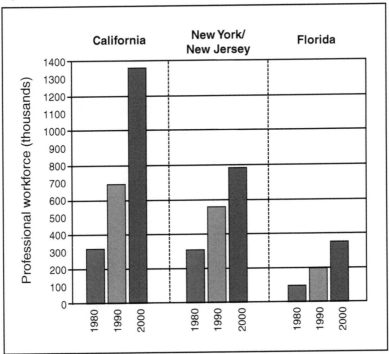

Source: Data obtained from U.S. Bureau of the Census, Public Use Micro-data. Sample 1980, 1990, and Current Population Survey 2000. Graph original.

The visual presentation here would enable a writer to point out that a greater number more immigrants in California had entered the professional workforce than in New York or Florida, a phenomenon that could than lead to an analysis of causation.

Pie Charts

Another useful way to present information is in the form of a pie chart, a visual representation that shows how a whole or a "pie" is divided. Pie charts are effective when there are only a small number of pieces to the "pie" and when the *relationship* between those pieces is important. For example, suppose your thesis or dissertation were concerned with showing changes in major causes of death in the United States, comparing percentages in 1950 with those in 2003. Figure 7.4 shows that a higher percentage died of heart disease in 1950 than in 2003 but that in 2003, a higher percentage of people died of cancer.

Figure 7.4—Major causes of death in the United States

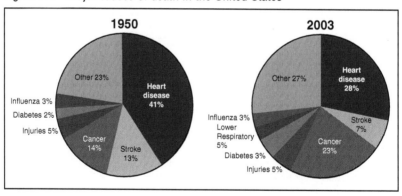

Source: Constructed from data in the National Center for Health Statistics, in public domain. National Center for Health Statistics, *Health, United States, 2005*.

The pie chart format is a more dramatic strategy for presenting comparisons and is much easier to read than two lists. It immediately attracts attention, making it easier for readers to "see" and compare differences in causes of death between the different years. For a writer, the pie chart provides a useful point of reference.

Line Graphs

A line graph illustrates the relationship between two variables. Usually, the independent variable is plotted on the horizontal axis and the dependent variable is plotted along the vertical axis. Line graphs are useful for showing how one variable influences another and for displaying trends in data over time. They therefore enable the writer to make predictions based on established trends. Figure 7.5, concerned with the percentage of people in the United States who smoke cigarettes, allows a reader to see that the percentage has gone down between 1965 and 2003.

Figure 7.5—Percentage of the U.S. population that smokes cigarettes

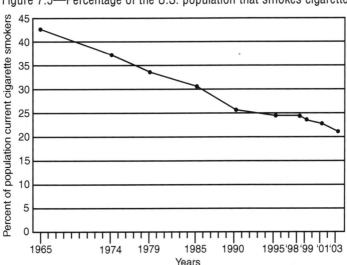

Source: Constructed from data obtained from the U.S. Department of Health and Human Services. Centers for Disease Control and Prevention. *Health, U.S. 2005.*

By tracing the line in the graph, a reader can see that that there has been a decrease in smoking over these years and can note the years in which the sharpest decrease occurred.

Line Graphs with Multiple Lines

As with bar graphs, line graphs can display more than one variable, making them particularly useful for showing comparative trends. Figure 7.6 shows changes in life expectancy between 1950 and 2005 for three different countries, Sweden, China, and Kenya. The lines highlight the fact that the life expectancy in China has continued to climb, whereas the life expectancy in Kenya has fallen, even though it rose from 1950 to 1985.

Figure 7.6—Changes in life expectancy since the 1950s

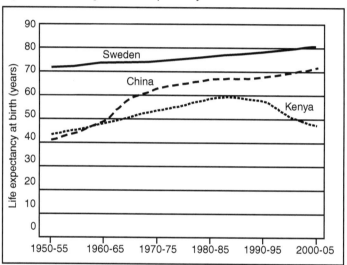

Source: Constructed from data obtained from The United Nations Population Division, World Population Prospects: The 2004 Revision.

The suggestions in this chapter are based on the idea that visual materials contribute to the argument of your thesis or dissertation but are not intended as a definitive discussion of various methods of data display. The most important point in this chapter is that visual materials fulfill an important *function* in developing your ideas and that awareness of that function will enable you to use visuals deliberately and insightfully.

Works Cited

Goggin, Maureen Daly. *Defining Visual Rhetorics.* Eds. Charles A. Hill and Marguerite Helmers. New Jersey: Lawrence Erlbaum, 2004.

Hill, Charles A. "The Psychology of Rhetorical Images." *Defining Visual Rhetorics.* Eds. Charles A. Hill and Marguerite Helmers. New Jersey: Lawrence Erlbaum, 2004.

The visual materials in this section were constructed by the author. They are based on information that is in the public domain.

8

The Advisor and Thesis/
Dissertation Committee

Every Luke needs a Yoda.
—http://icextra.ice.org.uk/tlml/everyluken

IN THE SECOND FILM in the *Star Wars* series, the hero, Luke Skywalker, in order to become a Jedi Knight, seeks the help of Yoda, an elflike creature with pointed ears. Yoda embodies the essence of good mentoring (despite his odd speech habits and pointed ears). He provides direction, support, and practical expertise, enabling Luke to gain confidence and, ultimately, independence.

Finding a good mentor, or "advisor," is an important element in writing a thesis or dissertation. Like Yoda, a good advisor provides guidance, direction, wisdom, support, and vision—all of which can enable you to grow as a student and scholar. However, advisors can vary in their mentoring abilities. A supportive advisor who takes the role seriously and understands its pedagogical, emotional, and political requirements can be an invaluable resource and become a lifelong colleague and friend. One who does not or who is so preoccupied with other commitments can make the process of writing a thesis/dissertation a challenge— sometimes a nightmare.

This chapter discusses concepts that you should be aware of when you choose an advisor for your thesis or dissertation.

It emphasizes the importance of student proactivity and involvement in forging a productive advisor/student relationship and is based on insights I wish I had understood when I was a graduate student.

Advisors and Mentors

The faculty member who works most closely with you in writing your thesis or dissertation is usually referred to as an "advisor," but sometimes he or she is called a "mentor." The terms are often used interchangeably, but for the purpose of this chapter, I distinguish them. The word *mentor* is Greek in origin and can be traced to Homer's *Odyssey*. Mentor was the name of Odysseus's friend who was given the task of caring for and educating Odysseus' son, Telemachus, when Odysseus went off to fight in the Trojan War. In the *Odyssey,* Mentor was essentially a teacher, and his job was to educate and instruct.

An advisor, in the context of graduate study, should do more than simply "educate" students. When you seek a primary reader or director for your thesis or dissertation, I urge you to focus on the term *advisor* rather than *mentor.* As R. W. Connell observes, "[s]upervising a research higher degree is the most advanced level of teaching in our education system." It is "one of the most complex and problematic" forms of teaching, and yet, "this complexity is not often enough acknowledged" (38). Although an advisor may indeed be a "teacher," someone with whom a student has taken a class, a productive advisor/student relationship is one that evolves beyond that of teacher/student, ultimately developing into a collaboration between colleagues.

This goal of becoming collegial partners suggests that although the initial relationship is between a teacher and a student, eventually the relationship develops to the point that the advisor and the student are working together. An effective advisor thus aims to foster a student's growth—in scholarship, professional development, and personal confidence. To accomplish these goals, he or she works in several arenas—not only the scholarly, but also the pedagogical, the political, and the psychological. As teachers and scholars, advisors enable graduate students to enter the scholarly conversation by introducing them to the discourse of scholarship within a particular discipline. But scholars are also writers, and advisors who are aware of writing pedagogy can help their students develop an effective writing process that will not only assist them in writing their thesis/dissertations, but also serve as an invaluable aid long after they receive their degrees. An advisor should also be a savvy departmental politician, aware of the necessity of helping students navigate the often treacherous political waters of department committees. Finally, although advisors may "criticize" work in progress, they often serve as cheerleaders and supporters, providing encouragement during the dark days when students feel tempted to give up and forget the whole enterprise. And there will be dark days—even very capable, successful students have them. As Christina Saidy, a student who wrote an excellent MA thesis, wrote:

> Forget the thesis
> I'll quit before beginning
> Who needs a masters?

In summary, then, "a committee chair must be strong enough to protect you and your work when the going gets tough and at the same time must be critical when the work is not up to acceptable standards" (Fitzpatrick et. al., 31). Until recently, little attention was given to the graduate student supervision relationship, which was "left to a traditional apprenticeship model, where the established 'master' inducts the new apprentice into the 'mysteries' of the craft" (Yeatman, 21). It is a model that no longer works, if it ever did, because it is "inadequate to the demands of a situation where many supervisees are barely socialized into the demands and rigours of an academic scholarly and research culture (Yeatman, 22).

Choosing an Advisor

Given the many functions that an advisor can play, you can see how important it is that you find out as much information as you can before choosing one and to think about what you need most. Is it most important for you to work with someone who has a reputation in his or her field and political influence in your department? Do you need access to particular data? Encouragement and support? Assistance in writing? Of course, ideally you would want someone who can provide everything you might need. But if you have to choose, which qualities in an advisor do you value the most?

In Chapter 1, "Getting Started," I suggested that you begin your search for an advisor early in your academic career, getting to know faculty members whose work is connected in some way with a topic you are considering for your thesis or dissertation. Getting to know these people and enrolling in their courses will help you decide whether you would like to work with them, as will reading their published works and familiarizing yourself with their "voices" in the scholarly conversation. I also suggested that you find out as much as you can about how these faculty members behave in an advising role. Some faculty members may be renowned scholars but are not particularly helpful to their graduate students. You have probably heard horror stories about advisors who are rarely available and who take many weeks, even months, to return drafts. Find out whether these horror stories are true, and seek any other information you can obtain from more advanced graduate students.

Kathy Leslie, the writer of a wonderful M.A. thesis, notes the importance of observing professors' habits in class. If the professor habitually hands back papers late, it is likely that he or she will not be prompt in handing back thesis chapters. Leslie also recommends becoming conscious of the kind of feedback the professor usually provides on course papers. Does the professor obsess about every mark of punctuation? Is he or she overly concerned with style? If so, will you be able to work with this person? Of course, if you are in a graduate program in which you did not take preliminary courses, you will not have this sort of previous experience.

Another point to consider is the extent to which a potential advisor will want to control your topic. Does this advisor tend to make suggestions and help students formulate ideas? Or does he or she have what Leslie refers to as a "great vision" of what your thesis ought to be? If so, are you willing to work with someone else's vision, or will you be butting heads throughout the whole process? To some extent, a thesis or dissertation should be balanced between a topic that you are excited to write about and one in which an advisor has at least some interest. If you insist on your particular topic or approach, you may have trouble finding an advisor who is willing to work with you. But if you simply accept a topic that an advisor recommends, you may become bored or angry that you have to write about something that doesn't particularly interest you. Another element to consider is whether you are planning to write a thesis or dissertation that departs from what is usually expected, perhaps a thesis or dissertation that adheres to a different format. If so, is your potential advisor supportive of this idea, and will he or she be willing or able to defend that choice against departmental resistance?

Another factor to consider is the professor's availability. Does the professor travel a lot? Does he or she return email messages promptly, come to the office frequently, and seem pleased to discuss ideas with students? Availability and willingness to meet with students are positive qualities. But is the professor so student-oriented that he or she is now directing too many theses or dissertations to give you enough time? These are all important factors to consider when deciding on an advisor.

Political Factors

Of course, you will want to work with someone with whom you have intellectual and emotional rapport. But it is also important to consider a professor's position in the department. You may have taken classes or seminars with a young assistant professor that you like a lot and whom you think would be an excellent advisor. However, in some instances, you might also want to consider how much influence that professor is likely to have with a thesis or dissertation committee because political elements can have a profound effect on your ability to complete your degree. When I was writing my dissertation, I first began working with a relatively young assistant professor with whom I had taken classes and who was genuinely interested in my dissertation topic. However, because the professor did not have a great deal of experience in directing dissertations, he did not fully understand the genre of the dissertation proposal—and, certainly, I didn't know very much about its requirements either. Consequently, although I thought I had written a well-focused proposal, I encountered difficulty in getting it approved by the department dissertation committee. Eventually, although this professor had become almost a friend, I decided to change advisors and selected someone who had been the chairman of the department and who knew his way around university committees. Within a month of changing advisors, I learned how to rewrite my proposal with attention to what the committee was "looking for," and my proposal was accepted. Then, as I muddled my way through the process of writing my dissertation, my new advisor was able to help me overcome any political roadblocks that arose. In my own case, then, the political element proved to be extremely important, and it is certainly something to consider when you are in the process of selecting an advisor.

As Yeatman notes, until recently, "the traditional mode of graduate student supervision has been governed by what Weber terms 'charismatic authority' (Weber, 295–97, cited in Yeatman, 21). The supervisee selects the supervisor on the basis of his charisma—that is, his extraordinary quality as a scholar.... And it works in two directions: in order for the charisma of the supervisor to prove to be worth believing in, the work of the supervisee has to be of a quality as to testify to the value of the supervisor's influence" (Yeatman, 22). This old model depended on notions of elitism and genius, and doesn't take into account the value of developing a working partnership between student and advisor.

Fostering a Collaborative Relationship with an Advisor

In "Professors as Mediators of Academic Text Cultures," Olga Dysthe points out that "professors represent the disciplinary culture and the discourse society into which the graduate student is being socialized, and the supervisor's conceptualization of the supervision relationship is of great importance for the interactions between the two about the student's text" (493–4). Dysthe discusses two models of "supervision": the monologic model, which "sees knowledge as a given," and the supervisor's role as that of transferring that knowledge to the student, and the dialogic model, which views knowledge as emerging from the interaction of voices and is concerned with the development of mutual understanding (500). Dysthe adheres to the dialogic model as the one most likely to produce a productive advisor/student relationship. When you select your advisor and begin working with him or her, you might consider which model you would prefer. Do you want to work "with" an advisor on a topic you consider worth pursuing? Or do you want to show up in your advisor's office and be told exactly what to do?

As a graduate student, you should be aware that although professors are usually well trained in their particular disciplines, they receive little or no training in supervision or advising; the skill of being an effective advisor is usually learned "on the job." As Anna Yeatman points out, "in the humanities and social sciences, the graduate student supervision relationship has been left to a traditional apprenticeship model, where the established 'master' inducts the new apprentice into the 'mysteries' of the craft" (21). In reality, though, the method tends to be unsystematic, constructed haphazardly on a "hit or miss" basis.

Because professors lack training in this area, they may simply imitate the advising model from their own graduate student days, a model that may not be well suited to your particular learning needs. Moreover, even when professors have a great deal of experience in directing theses and dissertations, their interactions and patterns of advising will vary according to the student being advised. Professors will work very differently with a confident student who comes to the office with clear ideas and gets right to work than with a pitifully insecure student who shuffles in without a clue about what he or she wants to do. Which kind of student are you? Perhaps, more important, which kind of student do you want to become? What sort of impression as a scholar and writer do you want to make on your advisor?

My point here is that you can have a significant influence over the sort of relationship you develop with your advisor by becoming conscious of your own needs and deciding on the "role" you want to play as you interact with your advisor and the members of your committee. Think of yourself as an emerging professional, not as a terrified student, and it is likely that you will be treated with greater respect by your advisor and members of your thesis/dissertation committee. Do you want your advisor to continue to function only as your "teacher," telling you what to do for every step of the process? Most students would not be comfortable with this sort of advisor, and advisors don't usually want this role, either. Of course, you don't want to come across as overly confident or arrogant, and unless you are unusually self-directed, you will probably not want an advisor who leaves you completely on your own—you will need advice and assistance at different intervals of the writing process. Aim to come across as confident and diplomatic as you set the tone for the developing relationship.

A Collaborative Partnership

How can you foster a productive working relationship that moves toward a collaborative partnership? Early conversations about ideas for your thesis or dissertation will help your advisor perceive you as a developing scholar and novice member of the discipline. If you have ideas about potential topics, by all means, discuss them during office conferences. You might also ask a possible advisor what he or she thinks are the most important research questions in the discipline or to suggest readings that can help you consider a topic in greater depth. Are there models of theses or dissertations that this particular professor thinks are worth examining? Does the professor expect you to write an annotated bibliography as a way to engage with significant readings? (This can be extremely helpful.)

You might also ask a potential advisor what supervision model he or she usually prefers. Will you be expected to submit each chapter as you write it? And (a more difficult, tricky question) how long does the advisor usually take to return submitted work? How frequently does the advisor like to meet? Is he or she interested in meeting with more than one graduate student at a time? Will you be expected to adhere to a timetable or plan?

Below are some questions you might want to ask a faculty member whom you are thinking of for your advisor. However, I caution you to be judicious in your questioning; no one wants to be bombarded with question after question. Keep these questions in mind and ask them respectfully as an opportunity arises.

- Do you expect your students to have a clear idea for a thesis or dissertation right from the beginning?

- What theoretical or methodological approaches do you think are most important?

- What do you consider to be the most important critical issues in the discipline?

- Do you have particular strategies for organizing and taking notes that you think are especially useful?

- Do you usually show students models of theses or dissertations that you think are especially successful?

- Do you usually instruct students about the components of a proposal and other elements in a thesis or dissertation, such as the review of the literature?

- Do you require students to write an annotated bibliography?

- How do you prefer to structure the writing process? Do you prefer students to submit each chapter as they write them? Or do you prefer to receive larger segments?
- What kind of feedback do you usually provide?
- Do you suggest articles, books, or other resources you think should be included?
- How do you recommend working with other members of a thesis/dissertation committee? Do you think students should submit a copy of each chapter to these members when they submit them to you? Or should they wait to submit a larger segment or a full draft?

Keeping a Graduate Student Log

To maximize the benefit of meeting with your advisor, I suggest that you keep a log or journal that summarizes what has been discussed during each meeting. Each entry need not be long or extensive—a one- to two-page entry written each time that one of these meetings takes place will suffice. Describe what occurred during the meeting—the focus of discussion in terms of both content and suggestions for improving the writing. Include a date for the next meeting and a short list of goals to be accomplished by that time. After composing each entry, send a copy to your advisor and encourage him or her to modify it as appropriate. The advisor will find this strategy helpful as well because it will allow him or her to recall what was discussed before the next meeting takes place.

When You Need to Replace Your Advisor

Occasionally, a graduate student may need to replace an advisor, a most unpleasant and emotionally stressful task. Perhaps the advisor has been promoted to a new administrative position and no longer has time to spend on a thesis or dissertation. Sometimes professors are so busy that they don't return phone calls or drafts of chapters. Sometimes the relationship just doesn't work, for personal or ideological reasons.

Fortunately, the need to replace an advisor doesn't happen very often. But if you find that your advisor is simply not working with you, it may be time for a replacement. How do you do this? Once again, proceed with caution, consulting people in your department who may have had experience in this matter. Fitzpatrick, Secrist, and Wright suggest that you write a letter, being as diplomatic and gracious as possible. Be respectful, citing the reason(s) for your decision politely and carefully. Although you may be tempted to vent your anger or disappointment in inflammatory statements, I urge you to refrain from doing so—do not burn any bridges. Some day this professor might be in a position of power that could affect your career.

The Thesis/Dissertation Committee

Selecting an advisor is an important decision. But the thesis/dissertation committee also has an important role.

Choosing Your Committee

In selecting other members of your committee, you likely will be limited by departmental requirements, and you may not have as much choice as you have in selecting your primary advisor. Still, I suggest that you consider the same factors for committee members as those for your advisor. Although second and third readers don't usually play as crucial a role as the primary advisor, I have heard of cases in which one member can significantly hold up the process of completing a thesis or dissertation. In one particularly horrendous case, a third member *permanently* prevented a graduate student from ever completing his degree! Fortunately, that rarely happens.

Working *with* Your Committee

The emphasis on the word *with* in the subtitle here calls attention to the diplomacy that is sometimes necessary when working with the various members of your committee and the importance of avoiding arguments, if possible. Each committee member might have a particular approach to your topic that he or she will want to see included, and sometimes these approaches can conflict. Or problems can arise between a graduate student and a committee member simply because of personal chemistry or just plain bad luck. But some of them can be avoided if you keep in mind the following three maxims:

1. Make sure that committee members remain aware of your existence.

2. Give committee members enough time to read drafts and suggest revisions.

3. Keep your eye on your ultimate goal: to complete your thesis or dissertation.

Maxim #1: Make Sure Committee Members Remain Aware of Your Existence

The extent to which each committee member is directly involved in the writing of your thesis or dissertation will vary according to your discipline, institution, department, and country; you should ask your advisor what sort of contact with other committee members he or she recommends. David Sternberg recommends that a candidate present his or her unfolding work "chapter by chapter, for approval to as many committee members as possible (again, preferably to all of them, but always to the advisor and second most interested faculty member)" (139), but I don't necessarily agree with that recommendation. A developing first draft may need considerable revision, and an advisor may prefer that you make necessary changes before submitting your work to other members of the committee. My own policy for advising is to work with my students through several drafts; only then do I suggest that they give a copy to other readers. Most second and third readers do not want to read drafts in a relatively unfinished stage.

Whether or not you submit chapters or early drafts to committee members, it is important that you stay in touch with them. Some graduate students become so immersed in research and writing that they disappear from the department, showing up again only when they need their work read or a signature on a form. Sometimes students are unwilling to show their developing work to anyone, except perhaps to their advisors, an understandable reluctance. However, it is really important that you keep committee members aware of your existence and remain a citizen of your department. Phone calls, emails, and brief visits to discuss progress will maximize committee members' interest in your project. In contrast, if you have "disappeared" from the department and then suddenly thrust a "completed" thesis or dissertation into committee members' hands with a request to read it and get back to you in a few days, you are likely to generate hostility and resistance—sometimes refusal.

Maxim #2: Give Committee Members Enough Time to Read Drafts and Suggest Revisions

Maxim #2 may seem self-evident, but graduate students sometimes have been working so closely with their advisors that they forget about obtaining input from other committee members. As you keep in touch with your committee, ask the members when they would like to receive drafts and how much time they would like before getting back to you. Also make sure that you have left enough time for yourself to make perhaps unanticipated revisions. Each member is likely to have at least a few suggestions, and I strongly encourage you to take their advice as best you can. This is not the time to stamp your feet and refuse to do as you are asked. Unless a suggestion is blatantly antithetical to your beliefs, goals, ethics, and scholarly integrity, I do not recommend saying, "I don't want to make this change because it would seriously compromise my ideas." If you have reservations about suggestions from other members of the committee, discuss them with your advisor and work out some form of negotiated approach. It is the advisor's job to help you deal with potentially difficult committee members, so do not attempt to do this on your own. As a graduate student in the process of completing a thesis or dissertation, you are at a vulnerable stage in your career, and it is important that you not put yourself in jeopardy before your work is signed and filed.

Maxim #3: Keep Your Eye on Your Ultimate Goal: to Complete Your Thesis or Dissertation
Negotiating your revisions will enable you to fulfill maxim #3— that is, to finish the thesis or dissertation and get your degree as expediently as possible. In this context, it is important to remind yourself that your thesis or dissertation does not have to be perfect. It is not your *magnum opus,* or your life's work. Do what is necessary to earn your committee's approval; if you want to make changes to it after you graduate, you will have the opportunity to do so without jeopardizing the possibility of receiving your degree.

The worst story I ever heard in this context concerned a friend of mine whose third reader wanted him to make certain changes to his dissertation. Because he didn't agree with those suggestions, he decided to eliminate this member from the committee in favor of another one who, he thought, would be more sympathetic to his original approach. To his surprise and consternation, the new third member also refused to approve the dissertation (for different reasons). Even worse was that his particular university had a "two strikes" rule that prevented my friend from ever completing his degree, despite appeals and potential lawsuits. Needless to say, this was a terrible blow to his career, and I continue to question the ethics of this decision. Don't let something like this happen to you. Maximize your chances for completing your degree—that is, present yourself as pleasant, respectful, intelligent, professional, concerned, hardworking, and attentive to detail, but not bothersome, arrogant, or stubborn. Do what is necessary to navigate suggestions for revisions and enlist your advisor to help you decide what to do if there are conflicting opinions. Remember, the goal is to finish the degree, not to write the culminating work of your life.

With your eye on the final goal, remember that persistence will ultimately win the day. If one of your committee members or your advisor severely criticizes your work, do not give in to despair and say, "Forget it. I might as well give up." Instead, express gratitude for the input, clarify uncertainties, make the necessary revisions, and resubmit the text—promptly. If it still needs further revision, make those revisions and resubmit. If you keep revising and resubmitting, you will eventually manage to fulfill the necessary expectations, and then—oh, glorious day—you will be finished!

> Free at last, I smile,
> Read for fun, sit in the sun.
> Thesis? What is that?
>
> —Ronit Sarig

Works Cited

Connell, R. W. "How to Supervise a Ph.D." *Vestes*. 2 (1985): 38–41.

Dysthe, Olga. "Professors as Mediators of Academic Text Cultures." *Written Communication*. 19.4 (October 2002): 493–544.

Fitzpatrick, Jacqueline, Jan Secrist, and Debra J. Wright. *Secrets for a Successful Dissertation*. Thousand Oaks: Sage Publications, 1998.

Sternberg, David. *How to Complete and Survive a Doctoral Dissertation*. New York: St. Martin's Griffin, 1981.

Weber, Max. "The Social Psychology of the World Religions." In *From Max Weber*. Eds. H. H. Gerth and C. W. Mills. London: Routledge and Kegan Paul, 1948.

Yeatman, Anna. "Making Supervision Relationships Accountable: Graduate Student Logs." In *Postgraduate Studies/Postgraduate Pedagogy*. Eds. Alison Lee and Bill Green. Sydney: Center for Language and Literacy: University of Technology, 1998. 21–30.

9

⎯⎯⎯◆⎯⎯⎯

Working with Grammar and Style

You can write in any way you like; it's a free country. But it's useful to know how readers are likely to react to your choices.
—Joseph M. Williams. *Style: Ten Lessons in Clarity and Grace.* Sixth edition. New York: Longman, 2000. vi.

MANY STUDENTS FEEL a shiver of apprehension when they hear the word *grammar,* particularly if it emerges from the curled lips of an English teacher. They associate the term with papers covered in mysterious red marks or with difficult and/or boring exercises assigned in high school. They consider "grammar" as something they "ought" to know, something they should have learned a long time ago and that "good" writers have somehow mastered. If you ask students, even graduate students, what they need to do to improve their writing, many are likely to respond, "Learn something about grammar." Even though many, many studies have demonstrated that grammar instruction, on its own, does not lead to writing improvement, there is a general view that learning grammar is a necessary prerequisite for becoming an effective writer. Periodically, educators and politicians call for additional grammar teaching as the solution to a variety of literacy-related problems.

The word *style,* on the other hand, tends to be associated with writing that is *not* bound by rules and school-related tasks.

Presumably "creative" writers and artists have "style," the implication being that style is linked with an author's personal identity. Style is often regarded as an artistic gift or is associated with a particular culture, as in the style associated with rap music. Unlike grammar, which presumably can and should be "learned," style is regarded as appearing without effort—some writers have it; others do not.

Neither of these beliefs is true, and neither can help you write your thesis/dissertation more effectively. As Martha Kolln maintains...

> [T]o be effective...writing [also] requires attention to rhetoric—and here is where the adjective *rhetorical* comes into the picture. Rhetoric means that your audience—the reader—and your purpose makes a difference in the way you write on any given topic. To a great extent that rhetorical situation—the audience, purpose, and topic—determine the grammatical choices you make. (2)

This perspective does not mean that grammatical "correctness" is irrelevant or that developing an appropriate style is unimportant. Rather, it argues that "grammar" and "style" are inextricably connected to rhetorical purpose, which, in this book, means entering a scholarly academic conversation in order to complete a thesis/dissertation. This "rhetorical" goal requires you to pay attention to the needs of your intended audience—that is, the scholars who are engaged in that conversation: your text-partners (see Chapter 2, "So What? Discovering Possibilities," for a further discussion of this term), your advisor, and your department committee. Those involved in this conversation expect to read texts that have a well-considered main point, are organized logically and coherently, adhere to established rules of punctuation and usage, and are written in an appropriately academic "style" that enables rather than inhibits comprehension.

With that goal in mind, this chapter uses a rhetorical approach to grammar and style and stresses the importance of using them to achieve your purpose: to write and complete your thesis/dissertation. It discusses some useful grammatical principles and stylistic strategies that you will be able to apply immediately to your own writing, focusing on the following topics: cohesion, coherence, emphasis, sentence expansion, and imitation.

Cohesion and Coherence

A well-written thesis/dissertation should have both cohesion and coherence, terms that are often considered to be alike but actually have different meanings when applied to written texts. *Cohesion* refers to interconnections or a sense of "flow" between sentences. *Coherence* refers to how a group of sentences, sometimes a paragraph, hangs together as a whole. Some writing may appear to be coherent because it seems cohesive—that is, one sentence seems to flow from one to the other. But the passage as a whole may not be coherent because it lacks unity and focus. Here is an example of such a passage:

> New York City is a wonderful place to visit in the winter. The snow accumulates in Central Park and gets very dirty sometimes. Dirty snow is not good for children to eat, as I was telling my niece the other day. But as usual, she was crying because she didn't have a new hat, and her mother was really irritated by her constant whining. Whining can get on anyone's nerves.

In this paragraph, each sentence connects with the one before and after. But the passage lacks a main point or focus because each sentence begins with a different topic—New York City, dirty snow, crying for a new hat, whining.

Cohesion

As a reader, you can easily discern when a group of sentences lacks cohesion. But what is it in these sentences that enable you to know this? And how can you apply that knowledge to your own writing? The principles and strategies discussed next will enable you to understand cohesion more deeply so that you can write more cohesively.

Meeting Reader Expectations

In speech or in writing, each statement sets up expectations for the statement that one expects will follow. If a friend greets you with the statement "The weather is terrible" and follows it with "Penguins live in Antarctica," you will, of course, be puzzled—perhaps alarmed. In speech, however, if a subsequent remark has little or nothing to do with a previous one, you can say, "What?" or "Wait, what does that have to do with what you said before?" But in writing, a reader does not have that option, and it is up to the writer to make sure that expectations are met. If the writer does not do so, the text lacks *cohesion*. We perceive that the earlier paragraph lacks cohesion because as we process one sentence, the next one does not meet our expectations. The first sentence, "New York City is a wonderful place to visit in the winter," sets up the expectation that the next sentence will provide an explanation of "why" New York City is wonderful to visit in winter. Instead, it refers to dirty snow—certainly not something we regard as wonderful.

This sort of disconnection is obvious in this passage because each sentence discusses a completely different topic. But thwarted expectations can also occur less obviously, even when the topics actually are connected thematically. For example, examine the two following sentences. Which one do you perceive as having more cohesion?

1. The gray cat sat near the fire, cleaning its paws. A very expensive pet shop was where the cat was purchased.

2. The gray cat sat near the fire, cleaning its paws. The cat was purchased from a very expensive pet shop.

Most likely, you perceive sentence #2 as the more cohesive because you expected the second sentence to say something about the cat before mentioning where it was purchased. Sentence #1 thwarts our expectations by stating something about the expensive pet shop before referring to the cat. The idea to remember here is this:

It is easier for a reader to process information when previously known information is presented *before* new information is added.

The first sentence provided information about the existence of a cat by the fire cleaning its paws, and our expectations are that the next sentence will pick up the idea of the cat and then add new information. Martha Kolln refers to this principle as the "known-new contract."

As an example of how the known-new contract promotes cohesion between sentences, read this passage written by James Williams on the subject of grammar:

> The grammar that most teachers know, the grammar of most handbooks, the grammar that gets taught in our schools, is known as *traditional grammar. Traditional grammar*—which is often called *school grammar*—can be recognized by its emphasis on grammatical terminology, such as the eight parts of speech, and by its emphasis on correcting errors. (318)

Note that the term *traditional grammar* in the first sentence is used to begin the second sentence, which elaborates on how traditional grammar can be recognized. "Traditional grammar," which was the new information in the first sentence, thus becomes the known information in the second.

Many writers use this strategy intuitively to create cohesion. But some do not, and it is helpful to be aware of how connections between known and new information fosters cohesion in a text so that you can apply the principle, when necessary. This principle, however, is not absolute and does not pertain in every case. Sometimes a cohesive link can be implied because the audience is so familiar with the subject that he or she can make the necessary connection. For example, in an email message to a friend, you may write:

Sally threw a fit today. Two-year-olds can be really difficult.

The implication here is that your friend knows that Sally is 2 years old, so the linking information (Sally is 2 years old) does not have to be provided. Or else you may wish to confound readers' expectations deliberately, to make a point or give emphasis.

But if readers are having difficulty understanding what you write and if you habitually receive papers back with "awk" written in the margins, you may wish to check your sentences for connections between known and new information.

Discourse Signals

Another technique that fosters cohesiveness is the use of "discourse signals," such as *for example; in the first place, second place; finally; in contrast;* and many other transitional expressions that help readers understand where you are heading. Academic prose is often filled with expressions such as *therefore, however,* and *in fact* that enable readers to make connections between ideas. Perhaps you already use them, but if not, it will be useful to think about where they might help you forge tighter linkage between ideas.

Parallel Structure

The use of parallel expressions to link sentences also fosters cohesiveness. Here is an example:

> Word processing, which enables infinite revision of texts, provides both advantages and disadvantages for writers. *It is easier* now than ever before for writers to revise their work before they submit it for publication. *But it is also harder* for writers to resign themselves to a completed product. Many are never satisfied, continuing to revise well beyond the point of improvement.

The paragraph by James Williams, cited earlier, also makes use of parallel structure in his first sentence to define "traditional grammar":

> The grammar that most teachers know, the grammar of most handbooks, the grammar that gets taught in our schools, is known as *traditional grammar.*

Exercise: Examine a section of your thesis/dissertation for examples of the known/new contract, discourse signals, and parallel structure between sentences. Try to rewrite a portion using these cohesive techniques.

Coherence

Whereas *cohesion* refers to linkages *between sentences, coherence* refers to a sense of focus both *within and beyond the paragraph,* as well as to the entire text. It requires not only cohesion between sentences, but also a sense of unity and linkage based on what a whole passage or chapter is about. Joseph Williams distinguishes between cohesion and coherence as follows:

> Think of cohesion as the experience of seeing pairs of sentences fit neatly together; the way two Lego pieces do.
>
> Think of coherence as the experience of recognizing what all the sentences in a piece of writing add up to, the way lots of Lego pieces add up to a building, bridge, or boat. (83)

Williams maintains that "readers judge a passage to be coherent when the words beginning each sentence cumulatively constitute a limited and related *set* of words. Those words are usually subjects of sentences, but not always" (84). Here is an example of a paragraph in which relationships between topics are indicated by repetition:

> In the United States, <u>dogs</u> are often treated as if they were <u>human</u>. In pet shops across the country, the <u>dog section</u> tends to be heavily stocked, not only with the expected items such as leashes and collars, but also with luxury items such as ivory-handled brushes, fruit-scented shampoos, and stylish outfits that, at first glance, one might think are intended for <u>human beings</u>. Moreover, dogs are now recognized as having psychological or emotional problems, similar to yet different from those of <u>human beings</u>. These problems must be treated by <u>dog psychologists</u> who are specially trained to understand the delicate <u>canine</u> psyche. Because Americans treat their <u>dogs</u> as well as, if not better than, they treat <u>human beings</u>, sometimes better than members of their own families, many American <u>dogs</u> live exceedingly comfortable, luxurious lives.
>
> Furthermore, in addition to buying expensive "doggie" products and providing the best of care, many Americans express great <u>physical affection</u> for their <u>dogs</u>, not only stroking them lavishly throughout the day, but also murmuring endearments and/or kissing <u>them</u> passionately on their silky ears.

The use of topic sentences, which are often but not always positioned at the beginning of a paragraph, helps create coherence. Often the topic sentence is at a higher level of generality than the sentences that follow, as in the paragraph about dogs, which makes the statement "In the United States, <u>dogs</u> are often treated as if they were <u>human</u>." The sentences that follow then develop the statement in some way, providing examples of how dogs are treated. The topic sentence in the next paragraph links to the main ideas in the first paragraph and then expresses another general topic: physical expression of affection.

Exercise: As you continue to read professional journals, focus your attention on how paragraphs are developed. Does each have a topic sentence? How are transitions used? What techniques enable you to perceive them as both cohesive and coherent? Can you use some of these devices in your own writing?

Emphasis

The Emphasis Principle

In writing your thesis/dissertation, you will, of course, want to emphasize particular ideas. Here is where your understanding of grammar and style can enable you to do so. My colleague Rei Noguchi urges writers to use what he refers to as the Emphasis Principle, which he defines as follows:

> To create emphasis, place the key idea *last* or in some other prominent position. (23)

What is meant by emphasis? Noguchi defines it as a key idea and advocates placing it in a final position in a sentence so that the reader will perceive it as important. To understand the Emphasis Principle, examine the following sentences:

1. Students completed a critical reading survey in their writing classes during the fall semester.

2. During the fall semester in their writing classes, students completed a critical reading survey.

3. Students completed a critical reading survey during the fall semester in their writing classes.

These sentences all have pretty much the same meaning. But they differ in the idea that is emphasized *based on what is placed last*. Many students are under the impression that a main idea should come at the beginning of a sentence. But that is not necessarily true. Positioning a main idea at the beginning of a sentence often results in flat, non-emphatic writing, which, as Noguchi phrases it, is "like telling your best jokes with the punch line first" (24).

Note that Sentence #1 emphasizes *the fall semester,* whereas Sentence 2 emphasizes *critical reading survey* and Sentence 3 emphasizes *writing classes.*

In other words, these three sentences answer different questions:

Sentence #1 answers the question "*When* did students complete a critical reading survey?"

Sentence #2 answers the question "*What* kind of survey did students complete during the fall semester?"

Sentence #3 answers the question "Where did students complete their critical reading surveys?"

It would be awkward if one asked the question "*What* kind of survey did students complete during the fall semester?" (#2) and the response was "Students completed a critical reading survey in their writing classes during the fall semester" (#1). Similarly, it would be equally awkward if one asked the question, "When did students complete a critical reading survey?" (#1) and the response was, "During the fall semester in their writing classes, students completed a critical reading survey" (#2).

As in the placement of new/old information, many writers have an intuitive sense of where to position a key idea in a sentence. But some writers do not, and, under the pressure of writing a thesis/dissertation, even good writers may misposition an idea, missing an opportunity to emphasize something important.

Active and Passive Constructions

The deliberate use of active or passive constructions is another way to achieve emphasis. "Active" constructions are those in which the subject of a sentence performs the action, as in "John painted the house." Passive constructions are those in which the subject of the sentence is acted upon, as in "The house was painted by John." Generally, energetic writing is associated with active constructions, but sometimes particular disciplines prefer one construction over another. Some counsel against writing in the passive, while others prefer it.

In the context of achieving emphasis, it is important to realize that the decision to use passive versus active constructions depends on what one wants to accentuate. For example, look at the following sentences:

1. The buyer was concerned about who had written the contract. The real estate broker wrote it.

2. The buyer was concerned about who had written the contract. It was written by the real estate broker.

Because the first sentence in these examples focuses on who wrote the contract, the second sentence should emphasize that. Therefore, this information should be placed in the latter half of the second sentence in order to achieve the greatest emphasis. In this example, then, the passive construction is the better choice.

What Noguchi refers to as the Emphasis Principle not only improves the effectiveness of sentences, but it also can extend to the organization of paragraphs and whole chapters. Suppose a writer wanted to write a paragraph about why graduate students often experience difficulties writing a thesis/dissertation proposal and had three reasons to offer: 1. A proposal is unlike other school-oriented assignments, 2. The nature of the proposal is difficult to define definitively, and 3. Students often have misconceptions about the necessity for originality.

What is the best sequence for presenting these three reasons in a paragraph? The Emphasis Principle, as defined by Noguchi, suggests "an ascending order based on importance"—that is, the most important reason or the one that the writer wished to emphasize, would be positioned last. If the writer wished to develop these ideas over many paragraphs, the same principle would pertain. Thus, the recommendation to place the most important idea last in order to achieve emphasis pertains at the sentence, paragraph, and whole text levels.

Emphasis Achieved Through Short Sentences

Because academic prose usually consists of long, complex sentences, a short sentence effectively positioned will attract a reader's attention. The use of strategically placed short sentences, then, is another technique you can use to achieve emphasis. Short sentences are used in this way in the following paragraphs. Locate these sentences, noting how they are used for emphasis and how they relate to the main point of the paragraph.

1. *The Devil Wears Prada* tells a familiar story, and it never goes much below the surface of what it has to tell. Still, what a surface! Bright and crisp and funny, the movie turns dish into art—or, if not quite into art, then at least into the kind of dazzling commercial entertainment that Hollywood, in the days of George Cukor or Stanley Donen, used to turn out. (Denby, David. "Dressed to Kill." *The New Yorker.* July 10 & 17 2006. 90.)

2. Some of the first studies of day care in the 1970s indicated that there were no ill effects from high-quality childcare. There was even evidence that children who were out of the home at an early age were more independent and made friends more easily. Those results received wide attention and reassured many parents. Unfortunately, they don't tell the whole story. "The problem is that much of the day care available in this country is not high quality," says Deborah Lowe Vandell, professor of educational psychology at the University of Wisconsin. The first research was often done

in university-sponsored centers where the child-care workers were frequently students preparing for careers as teachers. Most children in day care don't get such dedicated attention. (Wingert, Pat and Barbara Kantrowitz. "The Day Care Generation," *Newsweek,* Special Issue, 1990.)

Strategic Use of Punctuation Marks

Punctuation marks are usually thought of in terms of "correctness," and, of course, it is important to learn to use them correctly. This is the time to make the effort to learn a few rules about usage so that you don't submit your thesis/dissertation with surface errors that could distract or prejudice your readers, preventing them from focusing on your ideas or discoveries. I suggest that you keep a handbook available as you write so that you can check where to position that comma or quotation mark. Handbooks are also useful for checking citation and bibliographic conventions, which are so difficult to memorize and are constantly changing. This information is also easily available online through various university writing center websites; I especially recommend the On-line Writing Lab (OWL) at Purdue University.

Aside from their importance in making your text comprehensible, marks of punctuation can be used to achieve particular effects, enabling you to emphasize certain ideas. Here are some examples.

The Semicolon

The semicolon is used to link related ideas that otherwise would be stated in two sentences. Academic prose often contains a number of sentences that are linked this way. But a semicolon can also be used to create a bit of a pause that cannot be achieved if the sentences were linked with coordinating conjunctions such as *but, and,* and *for.*

Here is an example:

Debra bought a new dress for the wedding; Ellen refused to attend.

The sentence could have been written

Debra bought a new dress for the wedding, but Ellen refused to attend.

However, the use of the semicolon in the first sentence provides just the hint of a pause, giving a focus to the second sentence that is softened by the use of *but* in the second sentence.

Here is another example:

1. The general public believes that student writing problems can be solved with additional grammar instruction; no study has supported that belief.

2. The general public believes that student writing problems can be solved with additional grammar instruction, but no study has supported that belief.

Can you discern the difference between these two sentences?

Parentheses and Dashes

Parentheses and dashes can also be used for emphasis. Parentheses can be used to present an idea as a slight digression from the main point of a sentence or as a special idea that is shared between writer and reader. Here is an example:

Grammar (always certain to generate controversy among teachers) is best taught in the context of rhetoric.

In this sentence, the material enclosed in the parentheses can be read as a side commentary that the writer wants to insert into the conversation. If you imagine a scene in which someone is arguing for grammar being taught in the context of rhetoric, the parenthetical enclosure of the words "always certain to generate controversy" suggests that the speaker has placed her hand at the side of her mouth, confiding the idea as an *aside,* perhaps even whispering it.

However, if you want to *emphasize* the fact that grammar is always certain to generate controversy, you might want to use paired dashes. Here is how that sentence would then look:

Grammar—always certain to generate controversy among teachers—is best taught in the context of rhetoric.

Expanding Sentences

In grade school or high school, you probably learned that the core of a sentence consists of two components, the **subject** and the **predicate.** The subject, as one would suppose, can be defined as the person or thing that the sentence is about. The predicate is the point that is made about the subject or the action that the subject performed. Both the subject and the predicate can consist of only one word, as in the sentence "Dogs bark." In this sentence, the subject consists of the noun *dogs,* and the predicate consists of the verb *bark.*

In most sentences, and particularly in sentences contained in theses and dissertations, the subject and the predicate consist of many words. When the subject is comprised of several words, it is known as a noun phrase, which can be defined as "a group of words that acts as a unit" (Kolln 8), in which the main word is a noun. When the predicate is comprised of several words, it is known as a verb phrase, which can be defined as a group of words that acts as a unit in which the main word is a verb. Here are a few examples of simple sentences that clearly show these main two parts of a sentence:

1. The roof leaked steadily. (subject: *the roof;* predicate: *leaked steadily*)

2. Labrador retrievers are good pets. (subject: *Labrador retrievers;* predicate: *are good pets*)

3. John's grandfather grew a long white beard. (subject: *John's grandfather;* predicate: *grew a long white beard*).

Another definition to recall is that a sentence can also be defined as an independent clause if it consists of a subject and a predicate and functions independently. (If you did not enjoy grammar instruction when you were a child or adolescent, you are probably starting to shudder right now.)

Why is it useful to think about subjects, predicates, and independent clauses? Because you can expand sentences to achieve a more complex writing style by learning how and where to insert additional information.

Sentence Openers

The core of a simple sentence consists of a subject and a predicate, but writing that consists of all simple sentences sounds childish and unsophisticated. It is therefore useful to consider where in a simple sentence one might insert additional material. A particularly useful place, or, as Kolln refers to it, "slot," is at the beginning of the sentence. For example, the simple sentences noted previously could easily be expanded as follows:

1. *During the torrential rain,* the roof leaked steadily.

2. *Because they are gentle with children,* Labrador retrievers are good pets.

3. *To play Santa Clause in the Community Center Christmas pageant,* John's grandfather grew a long white beard.

Even from this brief illustration, you can see that there are infinite possibilities for expanding sentences through the "opener" slot. For academic writing, the opener slot is very useful for connecting two ideas using words that establish linkage, such as *however, therefore,* or *similarly; for example;* or phrases that establish connection. The following are several examples of how the "opener slot" can accomplish this:

The notion of personal voice was an important concept during the early days of the writing process movement. *However, eventually,* it came under attack as promoting a form of anti-intellectualism.

Read these sentences aloud, noting how the words *however* and *eventually* serve to connect the second sentence with the first. Then read them aloud, omitting those two words.

(The previous sentences discussed how computers can help students input and revise text) *In addition to enabling ease of text movement,* computers can also help with grammar and style. *For example,* students can consult on-line Writing Labs (OWLS) or websites that offer help with sentence structure, word choice, and grammatical issues.

The development of word processing software in the late 1970s marked the first and most pervasive influence of computers on composition. *In the mid-1970s,* I was writing my doctoral dissertation on a yellow pad, typing up my notes each night on an electric typewriter and laying the typed ages across a table, where I revised them with scissors and tape.

Other Slots for Expanding Sentences

In addition to the opening slot of a sentence, the middle and end slots provide places where you can add information to expand your sentences. Here are the simple sentences discussed earlier, with additional material added in the end slot:

1. The roof leaked steadily, *distracting Clara from her work.*

2. Labrador retrievers are good pets *because they are gentle and affectionate.*

3. John's grandfather grew a long white beard, *which made him look very much like Santa Claus.*

Here are the same sentences with material added in the middle slot (between the subject and verb).

1. The roof, *desperately in need of repair,* leaked steadily, distracting Clara from her work.

2. Labrador retrievers, *increasingly popular in the United States,* are good pets because they are gentle and affectionate.

3. John's grandfather, *who loved Christmas,* grew a long white beard, which made him look very much like Santa Claus.

The point here is that you don't have to be satisfied with sentences in their original form. Just because they happen to have emerged in a certain way doesn't mean that they have to stay that way. Play around with inserting information into various slots—as an opener, between the subject and the verb, or after the verb or predicate. Read your sentences aloud to get a sense of how one connects with another and to discern flow. Read the work of professional writers and scholars aloud as well. Note how sentences are constructed and try out different possibilities. Keep in mind that you can learn a style by studying its components and that the appropriateness of any style depends on its purpose and audience.

Imitation

The underlying messages of this chapter are that grammar and style are linked to purpose and audience and that understanding what makes writing effective will help you become a better writer. The ideas about cohesion, coherence, emphasis, and sentence expansion, discussed earlier, can help you develop as a writer, enabling you to complete your thesis/dissertation more successfully.

In this context, I also recommend that you find a piece of scholarly writing that you wish you had written and spend some time "imitating" it. The value of imitation as a learning strategy has, unfortunately, gone out of favor these days; particularly in the academic world, the usefulness of imitation is often distrusted, even disdained because it is associated with a "product" approach to the teaching of writing. It is presumed to squelch students' imaginations, resulting in lifeless, overly formalistic prose. In fact, the word *imitation* in composition scholarship is often preceded by the words *mere* or *slavish,* associated with something mechanical and stale.

I strongly disagree with these perspectives. Many established "creative" writers have acknowledged their early imitation of someone else's work and recall their attempts to capture the writing style of someone they admired as a stepping stone to acquiring their own. The ancient Greek and Roman rhetoricians, from whose insights the current field of rhetoric and composition has developed, were well aware that imitation is an important teaching and learning strategy, an important mechanism for attaining the flexibility and ease that facilitates experimentation. Certainly, the more recent "creative" writers who acknowledge their early debt to admired models eventually branched out from those models to develop their own styles. As Paul Butler argues, imitation "is a creative practice that has the paradoxical effect of liberating, rather than enslaving" (3).

I strongly urge you, then, to find the work of a scholar you admire and copy one or two paragraphs *by hand*. Of course, I realize that this statement must seem strange to you because writing by hand is not done very frequently—perhaps you haven't copied anything by hand since you were in grade school. But I think you will find that the act of actually copying someone else's writing will enable you to enter into it—that is, to understand its style with greater insight than if you had simply typed the text onto a computer.

After you have copied the text, examine it for the strategies of cohesion, coherence, emphasis, and sentence expansion, discussed earlier. Then try to adapt some of these strategies into your own work, using your own subject matter, of course. If you incorporate imitation into the writing of your thesis/dissertation, eventually the strategies you adopt will become your own—not exactly like the ones you imitated, but evolving into a style that is suited to your own rhetorical and professional goals.

The expectations for writing in a new genre are often hidden, remaining virtually invisible to those who haven't done it before. If English is not your first language, you will have the extra work of editing at the sentence level for appropriate word choice and grammatical correctness. Most universities, however, usually have a writing center or lab where you can obtain additional help with your writing; I also urge you to participate in a writing group that includes writers who are native English speakers.

Scrutinizing other theses and dissertations to understand how they are structured is also very helpful.

The ancient practice of imitation can foster awareness of unfamiliar text conventions and patterns, yielding valuable insights that can help you write more effectively. As the English poet Alexander Pope phrases it in "An Essay on Criticism":

> True Ease in Writing comes from Art, not Chance.
> As those move easiest who have learn'd to dance.

Works Cited

Butler, Paul. "Imitation as Freedom: (RE)Forming Student Writing." *NWP Publications*. (Spring 2002).

Kolln, Martha. *Rhetorical Grammar: Grammatical Choices, Rhetorical Effects*. Third Edition. Boston: Allyn and Bacon, 1999.

Noguchi, Rei. "Rethinking the Teaching of Grammar." *The English Record*. 52 No 2 (Winter 2002, 22–26).

Williams, Joseph M. *Style: Ten Lessons in Clarity and Grace*. Seventh Edition. New York: Longman, 2003.

10

Practical Considerations

24-pound bond!
Are they going to bench press it?
What does it matter?
—Kathy Leslie

IN THE PROPOSAL and drafting stages, a thesis or dissertation primarily involves thinking, research, and writing. But as you revise your work and envision a completion date, you have to pay attention to various requirements and rules, such as the necessity of using a specific weight and type of paper, which is mentioned disparagingly in the above haiku. Such requirements may indeed seem arbitrary and trivial, but each university has its own specifications and regards them very seriously. Therefore, it is important to figure out how to address them as efficiently as possible. This chapter focuses on practical elements associated with the thesis/dissertation process: writing the abstract, working with human subjects, and submitting a thesis/dissertation electronically. It also addresses the complex issue of plagiarism, which can cause a great deal of difficulty for any writer.

The Importance of Seeking Information Actively

The type of abstract you should write, the process of obtaining approval to work with human subjects, and the possibility of submitting your thesis/dissertation electronically are specific to your discipline and your institution. Therefore, I cannot provide you with all the information you might need about these considerations. The good news, though, is that this information is available to you through your university library and website, so if you are proactive in seeking information, you will find out what you need to know. The library will have examples of theses/dissertations that will help you understand what sort of abstract is most commonly written. Your university website will discuss requirements for obtaining approval for human subjects and information about the possibility or perhaps necessity of submitting your thesis/dissertation electronically. It will also list the various dates that each facet of the process is due.

To learn as much as possible about these requirements, I suggest that you ask advice from other students and, most important, that you consult with your advisor and any other member of the department who might have useful insights. The department secretary or graduate advisor can also be extremely helpful; often they are more knowledgeable than faculty members about Institutional Review Boards, procedures for working with committees, filing dates, necessary signatures, and a host of other matters. It is important that you maintain a friendly relationship with both of these people, treating them with respect and expressing gratitude—frequently—for any help they provide.

The main idea, then, is that you need to be an active seeker of information. As a graduate student aiming for a position in a college or university, you may think of yourself as a scholar—perhaps an absent-minded one, whose head is in the clouds. But to complete a thesis/dissertation successfully, you need to become earth-bound—that is, to become a practical person who doesn't miss deadlines or forget about requirements. Do not wait for someone else to provide you with necessary information or remind you when something is due. Focus on these practical considerations on your own.

Writing the Abstract

The abstract is an essential component of a thesis/dissertation; it also appears in most published research articles. Here is how the term *abstract* is defined by the American National Standards Institute:

> An **abstract** is an abbreviated accurate representation of the contents of a document, preferably prepared by its author(s) for publication with it. (78-79)

In the context of a thesis/dissertation, the purpose of an abstract is to give your readers a concise overview of the work you have done. Although the length and nature of an abstract will vary according to your discipline and institution, as a genre, it consists of the following elements:

- It states what the thesis/dissertation *does* or the *purpose* of the thesis/dissertation. This element may include a brief statement of why the study is being conducted or the rationale or problem that is being addressed.

- It explains briefly *how* the thesis/dissertation did it, or the *methodology* that was used.

- It indicates *what the author found.*

- It states *what the author concluded.* This element may also include the implications or significance of the study.

Approaching the abstract as a genre, as the word *genre* has been defined in this book, will focus your attention on its connection to purpose, writer, and audience. In this context, aside from the fact that the abstract is a necessary requirement for completing your thesis/dissertation, think about your goal in writing an abstract of your work. Who do you envision as your audience? Your advisor? Your committee? Other students? Scholars in the field? Someone on a search committee when you are on the job market? What impression of you and of your work do you want your audience to obtain from reading your abstract? What elements of the abstract will enable it to fulfill its purpose most effectively?

Having analyzed many abstracts in a number of disciplines, the linguist Vijay Bhatia maintains that an abstract should contain four "moves," a term that can be understood as a "direction" in which the text advances or as an element that proceeds in a particular sequence. You may recall that I used the term *move* in Chapter 4, "Mapping Texts: The Reading/Writing Connection," which was concerned with mapping texts. Bhatia conceives of the "moves" of the abstract as follows:

1. *Introducing purpose*

   This move provides the author's intention, main idea, or hypothesis, which constitutes the underlying purpose of the research. This move may also include a direct statement of the main goals or objectives of the research or problem.

2. *Describing the methodology*

   This move describes the design, procedures, or method that was used to conduct the research.

3. *Summarizing results*

   This move pertains especially to theses/dissertations that involve observations, discoveries, or solutions to a problem. It has particular relevance to theses/dissertations in which data has been collected.

4. *Presenting conclusions*

   This move interprets the results and suggests implications of the research.

The following several examples of abstracts illustrate the various moves Bhatia notes. Can you use one of these abstracts as a model for your own?

Abstract #1 is from a thesis that used surveys to collect information about students' familiarity with critical reading strategies among college freshmen. Note the various moves included in this abstract.

Abstract #1 (written by Sally Diessner)	Moves

Critical Reading Strategies of First-Year Composition Students: A Reading-Writing Connections Study

This thesis measures the use, non-use, and new use of critical reading strategies (CRS) among college freshmen or first-year Composition students.	*Move 1: Purpose*
Freshman at two universities completed a combined total of 691 "beginning-of-semester" and 534 "end-of-semester" surveys during the spring 2005 semester.	*Move 2: Method*
The study's statistical analysis reveals significant correlations between respondents' historical literacy backgrounds, reading-writing connections, and computer skills. A key finding is that a majority of respondents (ESL students, in particular) are either unfamiliar with or simply do not use 10 "advanced" college level critical reading strategies.	*Move 3: Results*
This result is highly relevant for both teachers and students across all disciplines because the use of CRS helps students become more proficient readers and interpreters of college-level texts, and ultimately better writers.	*Move 4: Conclusions and implications of the research*

Abstract #2 is from a thesis that used focus groups to investigate whether faculty in her university business school have a different concept of what constitutes good student writing than do faculty in her university English department.

Abstract #2 (written by Jennifer Johnson)   Moves

Tensions in the Writing Center

This thesis examined the perspectives of a group of   *Move 1: Purpose—*
Business faculty, a group of English faculty, and a   *also the rationale*
group of Writing Center consultants concerning   *for the purpose*
what constitutes good student writing. The impetus
for this study was the general perception in the university Writing Center that the Business faculty are
more concerned with surface correctness than are its
English faculty. This distinction, however, had not   *Move 2: Method*
been established definitively. Focus group methodol-
ogy was used as a means of determining the extent
to which this apparent disparity actually exists.
The study revealed that although emphasis on criti-   *Move 3: Results*
cal thinking and correctness of the final product
varied between the two disciplines, they seem to be
slowly moving closer to a more common ground.
Further investigation is needed to determine if the   *Move 4:*
results of this study pertain to the Business and   *Conclusions and*
English faculty at other universities.   *suggestions for*
    further research

Abstracts #1 and #2 are from theses that involve responses or
observations. Abstract #3 is from a thesis that analyzes cookbooks. It exemplifies an abstract that uses texts as the basis of
research and analysis.

Abstract # 3 (written by Kathy Leslie)   Moves

Deconstructing Betty Crocker: A Genre and Stylistic
Analysis of Cookbooks

This thesis undertakes a genre study of cookbooks to   *Move 1: Purpose—*
determine to what extent they construct and rein-   *also the rationale*
force feminine roles. Cookbooks are largely consid-   *for using a particu-*
ered as reference books and, as such, are thought to   *lar approach*
be free of ideology. However, genre theory provides a   *Move 2: Method—*
strategy of analysis that explains how texts both   *also an overview of*
reflect and construct social actions. It also provides   *how the project will*
insight into the ideologies and power structures   *be approached*

advanced by these texts. A brief history of cookbooks places them into historical and social contexts in order to show how roles are constructed and reinforced by these texts, how cookbooks envision and position the reader vis-à-vis the text, and how the genre is reflective of its place in history. A stylistic analysis of four individual cooking texts, each representative of a particular era, is performed in order to provide data on which to base conclusions about this genre. The thesis will contribute to the field of Rhetoric by demonstrating how these texts construct meaning and, in doing so, promote particular ideologies.

Move 3: Conclusions and implications of the study

You will note in Abstract #3 that because the author does not discuss her findings, that there are only three "moves," and you should keep in mind that there is no absolute formula for writing an abstract. Abstract #3 devotes several sentences to the rationale for the thesis. However, in Abstract #4, which is taken from the journal *Urban Affairs Review,* the abstract includes several sentences of background before the purpose of the study is explained but only one sentence that describes the methodology. Presumably, the author felt that the intended audience was not familiar with the term *rent-seeking* but was quite familiar with the use of *panel data.* In writing your abstract, of course, you need to consider the needs of your intended audience in terms of background and knowledge base.

Abstract #4 (written by Jason Kaufman)   Moves

Rent-Seeking and Municipal Social Spending:
Data from America's Early Urban-Industrial Age

The term *rent-seeking* refers to special interest group efforts to seek special benefits at little or no cost to themselves. Because government spending has the potential to create both costs and benefits for taxpayers, fiscal policy is commonly viewed as a primary arena of rent-seeking activity. At least five different

Move 1: Provides background on the topic

theories of nineteenth-century American urban development fit this general rubric. Each theory predicts different winners and losers as well as different underlying strategies and distributions of interests incumbent upon municipal decision making. This study uses two-wave panel data on special interest group representation and municipal social spending to examine the validity of these different theories of rent-seeking. **Though all such theories share in common an emphasis on self-seeking, this study points to the role of competition between different sectors of the local economy as a motivating force for the formation and mobilization of special interest group organizations.** This finding contrasts with those rent-seeking theories that predict widespread cooperation among communities and/or classes in pursuit of common goals. Suggestions for future research on this topic are offered as well.

Move 2: Method

Move 3: Results

Move 4: Conclusions and implications for further research.

Abstract #5 uses a straightforward sequence of moves that might be characterized as "Here is what people generally think is true. This study shows that their beliefs are incorrect." It begins with the rationale for the study: to examine the truth of what is generally believed about parents' sex preferences for children. The conclusion, noted in the final sentence, contradicts that perspective.

Abstract #5 (written by Gunnar Andersson, Karsten Hank, Marit Rønsen, and Andres Vikat.

Gendering Family Composition: Sex Preferences for Children and Childbearing Behavior in the Nordic Countries

Moves

It has been argued that a society's gender system may influence parents' sex preferences for children. If this is true, one should expect to find no evidence of such preferences in countries with a high level of gender equality. **In this article, we exploit data from population registers from Denmark, Finland, Norway, and Sweden to examine continuities and changes in**

Move 1: States what is generally believed

Move 2: Method

parental sex preferences in the Nordic countries during the past three to four decades. First, we do not observe an effect of the sex of the firstborn child on second-birth risks. Second, we detect a distinct preference for at least one child of each sex among parents of two children. For third births, Danish, Norwegian, and Swedish parents seem to develop a preference for having a daughter, while Finns exhibit a significant preference for having a son. **These findings show that modernization and more equal opportunities for women and men do not necessarily lead to parental gender indifference. On the contrary, they may even result in new sex preferences.**

Move 3: Results

Move 4: Conclusions and implications for further research

In writing your abstract, I suggest that you examine theses/dissertations that have been written by students in your department and, of course, that you consult your advisor about how much information you should include. Another useful strategy is to attempt to write your abstract *before* you have finished writing your thesis/dissertation. Although you may not yet have obtained definitive results, the process of attempting to write an abstract beforehand will focus your attention on your central purpose and remind you of the direction you want to pursue. You may discover that you have digressed somewhat from your original intentions or have moved in a completely different direction; it is better to discover this *before* you have written an entire thesis/dissertation that will have to be refocused.

Working with Human Subjects: Institutional Review Boards

Many theses/dissertations involve contact with people as a means of conducting research, and the U.S. Department of Health and Human Services (HHS) requires that such research be reviewed and approved by an Institutional Review Board (IRB). Every university has an IRB; some have several, one for the social sciences and one for the hard sciences. All are in compliance with HSS regulations, and all have the responsibility of protecting the rights of human subjects. It is extremely important that you become familiar with the requirements of the IRB at your institution and undertake the necessary steps to gain approval; if you don't, you can run into a great deal of trouble. Without IRB approval, your thesis/dissertation will not be accepted, and you may not receive your degree. Moreover, some journals will not publish research deriving from a thesis/dissertation unless indication of IRB approval is included with submission.

Here are some important definitions that you should become familiar within the context of gaining approval from an IRB.

Research

The federal rules define *research* as a systematic investigation, including research development, testing, and evaluation, designed to develop or contribute to generalizable knowledge.

Human Subject

A human subject is defined as anyone about whom an investigator conducting research obtains 1) data through intervention or interaction with the individual or 2) identifiable private information.

Human Subjects Research

Human subjects research is defined as research that involves the collection and analysis of data obtained from living persons. Policies that address human subjects research are designed to minimize risks to subjects, to protect subject confidentiality, and to ensure that subjects are informed about what sort of participation is involved, including any risks. This type of research might include interviews, observations, or reviews of records such as transcripts, surveys, or medical experiments.

Informed Consent

"Informed consent" means that participants have chosen to be involved in a study without being coerced, deceived, threatened, or otherwise influenced to participate. Information provided to participants should include the purpose of the research, potential risks and benefits, information about payment, and the right to refuse to participate.

Confidentiality

A component of informed consent is the assurance to participants that information provided will be kept confidential, a consideration for certain types of data that participants would prefer to remain private. Additional information should be provided to participants about potential plans for publication resulting from the study and information about what will happen to the data after the study has been completed.

Minimal Risk

This is a term that is often used in the context of classifying the sort of review required by a particular study. It means that the probability and anticipated degree of discomfort are not greater than those ordinarily encountered in the course of living or those associated with routine physical or psychological examinations.

Consider, then, the nature of the research that informs your thesis/dissertation. If it focuses only on texts, such as an analysis of library resources or literary works, you may not need a review by an IRB. You also might not need one if you are conducting research in an educational context, such as a project that is used in a classroom setting. But other types of research—even student data, surveys, and some classroom activities—might be subject to this type of review. Ask questions and check requirements frequently, as regulations can change.

Three Types of Review

Three types of review are done, depending on the nature of the research being conducted.

Exempt Review

This type of review pertains to studies that federal regulations have identified as "exempt" from Human Subjects Panel Review because they provide minimal risk. The research has been characterized as so harmless, nonintrusive, or common that there is little harm or risk to human subjects. Examples of "exempt" review might be those conducted in educational settings, such as classrooms, surveys or interviews, observations of public behavior, or studies existing data. Some institutions require a particular procedure for an exempt review, but the process is not complicated and does not involve constant monitoring.

Expedited Review

This type of review also does not involve serious risk to the population being studied. It is reviewed by a primary reviewer and is subject to continuing review. Some interviews, survey data, and short-answer questions fall under this category.

Regular Review

This sort of review does not usually pertain to research being conducted for a thesis/dissertation. In studies involving children, prisoners, or adults deemed incompetent, however, a more extensive, continuous review process may be necessary. A regular review may also be required if the information collected could place subjects at risk of criminal or civil liability if the information became known.

There is no question that gaining approval from an IRB can pose problems, but you can minimize potential difficulties if you frame your request for working with human subjects as thoughtfully and clearly as possible. Make sure that you include a clear statement of the purpose of your research, information about the methodology you plan to use, the population you are targeting, and the protection you will provide regarding risk and confidentiality. Some of this information is likely to be in the original proposal you wrote to get your topic approved by your department committee, and you will find it relatively easy to cut and paste from that text. In all aspects of the thesis/dissertation process, it is important that you demonstrate credibility, showing that you have the qualifications to conduct the intended research; this requirement is especially important when you are applying to an IRB. Be sure to cite references from refereed journals to show that you have probed your subject deeply, and maintain a careful, realistic tone. Even if you secretly believe that your research will transform the nature of civilization as we know it, the proposal to an IRB is not the place to make that statement. Provide as much information as necessary so that your audience can understand exactly what you plan to do, indicate your concern with avoiding risk to participants, and follow all recommendations carefully.

The following checklist applies to an IRB for working with human subjects:

- Check all requirements at your university and ask a lot of questions.
- Make a list of deadlines and be sure to meet them.
- Write your proposal with the goal of helping the IRB understand exactly what you are doing.
- Cite scholarly refereed journals and well-regarded books to indicate the depth of your research.
- Indicate your concern with avoiding risks to participants and maintaining confidentiality.
- Follow all recommendations carefully.

Electronic Theses and Dissertations (ETDS)

Increasingly, many universities and libraries are making digitized or electronic versions of theses and dissertations available, and some universities are beginning to require that all theses/

dissertations be submitted electronically. The idea for doing so was first discussed in 1987 at a meeting in Ann Arbor, Michigan. A representative from Virginal Tech University who was attending that meeting took the lead in making this option available for its students. There is now a growing Networked Digital Library of Theses and Dissertations (NDLTD), which was funded by a grant from the U.S. Department of Education. It is possible, then, that your university may encourage or require electronic submission. The next section discusses some issues associated with this option.

The Rationale for ETDs

According to Christian R. Weisser and Janice Walker, "electronic theses and dissertations, or ETDs, are defined as those theses and dissertations submitted, archived, or accessed primarily in electronic formats. That includes traditional word-processed (or typewritten and scanned) documents made available in Print Document Format (PDF), as well as less-traditional hypertext and multimedia formats published electronically on CD-ROM or on the World Wide Web" (www.press.umich.edu/jep/03-02/ etd.html). Advocates for electronic submission and membership in The Networked Digital Library of Theses and Dissertations (NDLTD) base their rationale on a number of considerations, among them ease of archiving, storage, and dissemination, as well as the increasing use of multimedia or hypertextual elements in theses/dissertations that are not easily represented in paper versions.

As Weisser and Walker note, "many theses/dissertations lie moldering in library basements, with no efficient way for researchers to locate the information that may be contained in them. Further, the time and costs involved in procuring copies of those works may often be prohibitive." Storing and accessing theses/dissertations electronically would thus be easier and cheaper than the current system, which depends on paper or microfilm. Information submitted electronically is easily saved, thereby minimizing information loss. Moreover, electronic documents will not be subject to the discoloration and disintegration characteristic of paper texts and would allow efficient online searching through the World Wide Web.

Weisser and Walker also point out that current theses/dissertations sometimes include multimedia elements, such as audio and video, hypertext links, or other hypertext elements. Most universities currently require those theses/dissertations to be submitted on paper, a requirement that can prevent the effective use of multimedia or that necessitates the submission of two versions, one paper and the other electronic. A move to electronic submission would thus enable students to incorporate multimedia elements and expand possibilities for experimentation with new forms.

Problems Associated with ETDs

In the context of the subtitle of this book, "Entering the Conversation," electronic access seems advantageous in that it would enable the "conversation" to be greatly expanded. With information from theses/dissertation readily available, anyone conducting research would be able to access information quickly and easily using online search capabilities. Moreover, researchers would be able to retrieve particular chapters or specific components without having to print the entire document. However, what must also be considered is that although an ETD might be easily accessed, reading a lengthy work online is difficult, and the cost of printing a paper copy could be more expensive than the current system of ordering one through University Microfilms International (UMI), which "publishes and archives dissertations and theses; sells copies on demand; and maintains the definitive bibliographic record for over [1/4] million doctoral dissertations and master's theses." (www.umi.com/hp/Products/Dissertations.html)

Other problems that need to be addressed include copyright issues and potential difficulties that occur when new versions of software no longer can accommodate files produced by older versions. Finally, some scholars might feel that even a completed thesis/dissertation must still be regarded as a work in progress because it has not been given the rigorous scholarly review required of well-regarded articles or books. Those who hold this perspective feel that worldwide distribution of theses/dissertations might lead to the dissemination of undeveloped ideas or misleading information.

As a graduate student currently in the process of writing a thesis/dissertation, you should find out whether you have the option of submitting your work electronically and consider whether you want to do so. Of course, your university may require you to do so, in which case you have to find out what the process involves. If electronic submission is an option or is required at your university, the Office of Graduate Studies will provide the information you need. You can also find up-to-date information at the National Digital Library of Theses and Dissertations (NDLTD) website (www.ndltd.org) and Virginia Tech's ETD website (etd.vt.edu/background).

Plagiarism and How to Avoid It

If you input the keyword *plagiarism* into a search engine such as Google.com, you will obtain an impressive number of sites that address the increased "problem" of plagiarism due to ease of access through the Internet. Many of these sites will also provide a number of suggestions about how to avoid plagiarizing, and I suggest that you follow these carefully. Although in some societies the necessity of citing everything may not be so important, the failure to do so at an American university will be regarded as plagiarism, which is considered a very serious offense. Of course, as a graduate student, you are no doubt aware of the importance of documenting all references to outside sources, to avoid inadvertently plagiarizing. However, in writing your thesis or dissertation, you have been working with many sources, and it is easy to forget to document something. Therefore, it is very important that you check your work carefully. A charge of plagiarism can have grim consequences for your academic and professional life, possibly preventing you from ever completing your degree.

A number of websites will help you avoid plagiarizing, among them the Purdue OWL (Online Writing Lab, http://owl.english. purdue.edu/owl/resource/589/01/), which is a veritable treasure trove of information about many issues associated with writing. Emphasizing that "the key to avoiding plagiarism is to make sure you give credit to where it is due," the site provides the following list of what needs to be documented or credited:

- Words or ideas presented in a magazine, book, newspaper, song, TV program, movie, web page, computer program, letter, advertisement, or any other medium
- Information you gain through interviewing or conversing with another person, face to face, over the phone, or in writing
- When you copy the exact words or a unique phrase
- When you reprint any diagrams, illustrations, charts, pictures, or other visual materials
- When you reuse or repost any electronically available media, including images, audio, video, or other media

The site recommends that you document any words, ideas, or pictures that do not originate with you.

The problem, though, is that it is sometimes difficult to decide when something is "common knowledge"—that is, generally known—or something that needs to be cited. In a beginning writing class, for example, a student may become acquainted with the term *discourse community,* a term that she didn't know before and that she feels she needs to cite. But as she immerses herself in her discipline, she will probably discover that the audience for which she is writing is well acquainted with that term and, therefore, that she doesn't need to cite it after all. My suggestion is that if you are in doubt, cite more than you think is necessary and consult your thesis/dissertation advisor about whether you need to do so.

Another way to avoid inadvertent plagiarism is to make sure that you keep careful notes and record the complete source, even if you are pressed for time. Use quotation marks around direct quotations, and credit paraphrases and summaries, checking what you have written against the original source. Although blatant cases of plagiarism receive a great deal of attention, both in the academy and in the media, most students don't plagiarize deliberately and would be horrified if they were accused of doing so. Pay attention to whose words you are using, and be as scrupulous as possible about the notes you take. As in so many other aspects of writing a thesis/dissertation, awareness and planning will help you avoid potential difficulties.

Conclusion

So you have completed multiple drafts of your thesis/dissertation, checked various requirements, and printed it on the appropriate paper. Finally, it is time to sit back, take a deep breath, and feel the pride of accomplishment lift your spirits. Writing a thesis/dissertation is not easy, but you did it—and it is now time to say "Congratulations!"

Works Cited

Bhatia, Vijay K. *Analysing Genre: Language Use in Professional Settings*. London: Longman 1993. 77–79.

The Journal of Electronic Publishing. December, 1997 Volume 3, Issue 2. www.press.umich.edu/jep/03-02/etd.html.

Index

Made in the USA
San Bernardino, CA
20 January 2020